Concerning E.M. Forster

CONCERNING E.M.FORSTER

FRANK KERMODE

Weidenfeld & Nicolson
LONDON

First published in Great Britain in 2009
by Weidenfeld & Nicolson

10 9 8 7 6 5 4 3 2 1

© Frank Kermode 2009

A CIP catalogue record for this book
is available from the British Library.

ISBN: 978 0 297 85116 5

Typeset by Input Data Services Ltd, Bridgwater, Somerset

Printed and bound in the UK by CPI Mackays, Chatham ME5 8TD

The Orion Publishing Group's policy is to use papers that
are natural, renewable and recyclable products and made
from wood grown in sustainable forests. The logging and
manufacturing processes are expected to conform to
environmental regulations of the country of origin.

Weidenfeld & Nicolson

Orion Publishing Group Ltd
Orion House
5 Upper St Martin's Lane
London, WC2H 9EA

An Hachette UK Company

www.orionbooks.co.uk

Contents

Introduction

The three chapters which form Part One of this book were given as the Clark Lectures in 2007. I must at the outset express my gratitude to the Master and Fellows of Trinity College, Cambridge for inviting me to give them and then entertaining me so splendidly.

Choosing E.M. Forster as my main topic was partly a matter of sentiment. Forster had served as Clark Lecturer in 1927. His lectures on the novel enjoyed a considerable popular success, which was augmented when they appeared in book form as *Aspects of the Novel* in the same year. While the lectures were still in progress he had the additional satisfaction of being elected into a Supernumerary Fellowship at King's, the college to which he had been admitted as an eighteen-year-old undergraduate in 1897. His association with King's, never seriously interrupted, was further strengthened when he became an Honorary Fellow in 1946. In that year he also accepted an invitation to reside in college – 'a quite unusual offer', as his biographer P.N. Furbank remarks. At first he was not sure whether he would enjoy living in college, and in the busy years that followed he was often absent from Cambridge, but from 1953 till his death in 1970 his home was in King's.

My relationship with King's was quite different. I graduated from Liverpool University in 1940 and returned there as a research student after the war, in 1946. In 1947 I went to Newcastle University – then a college of the University of Durham – as a lecturer, but in order to go on enjoying the influence of a Liverpool teacher, who in 1950 moved to a professorship at Reading University, I followed him there. My next moves, in 1958 and 1965, were to Chairs at Manchester and Bristol, but in 1967 I came to what I supposed might be the last of them, to the Lord Northcliffe Chair at University College, London. But this wasn't, after all, to be my last move, for I was in 1973 offered the King Edward VII Chair at Cambridge, and in the following year I was elected into a fellowship at King's College. Indeed I moved into college and for a year occupied a pleasant set of rooms looking across the back lawn to Clare, an agreeable sight in almost all weathers. I gave up that set and moved out, but remained a Fellow to retiring age in 1987, when I was granted an Honorary Fellowship.

I'm conscious that all this academic detail is tedious, but it seemed necessary to explain that my decision to talk about Forster had its origins in some transitory and fleeting resemblances or coincidences as well as in differences in class and education that would be reflected in my lectures. When I moved into King's in 1974 I had known Forster's novels for half a century, but I knew very little about Cambridge or the college, and that kind of knowledge I lacked was the kind that is acquired slowly, and preferably earlier in life. I was now in daily contact with men who had known Forster well – courtly, serious men who welcomed the newcomer but were not particularly interested in talking about Forster at a time of rapid change in the life of the college, which had only very recently begun to admit women students.

There are happily still some survivors, men who knew Forster when they were undergraduates and encountered him quite casually in the college or were asked to tea and even to accompany him on holidays abroad. Some claimed to have liked him extremely, and some did not. The most remarkable of these survivors is P.N. Furbank, Forster's biographer, the editor of his letters, and a great reservoir of information about Forster, with whom he was, to the benefit of all his readers, on familiar and affectionate terms.

I myself met the great man only once for ten minutes or so, I think in 1955. He was patient but understandably a little bored or tired, and I remember the conversation best because he told me that the caves in *A Passage to India* should be pronounced 'Marábar' and not 'Marabár'. As he explained in the notes he wrote for the Everyman edition of the novel in 1942, the name of the caves was adapted from that of the real Barabar Hills. He had visited Barabar in 1913, and the caves of the novel are imaginatively based on what he saw there – there is an elaborate description in Forster's letter to his mother, dated 25 January 1913 (*Selected Letters*, I. 183ff.). The main difference between Barabar and Marabar is that 'the caves on the Barabar are ... known to be Buddhist, and their entrances are not unornamented'. Furbank in his biography (I. 247n) says that Forster, much later, told him the caves were 'not all that remarkable ... until they got into his book'. As to my brief conversation with the master, it ended, I think, with an allusion to Forster's specialized use, in *A Passage to India*, of the word 'extraordinary', introduced in the first sentence of the novel. Then my time was up. From my point of view it was, I thought, quite well spent, though he would probably have judged it differently.

I have situated myself in Forster's college, but have so far omitted to explain how I came to be there – after all, there were a good many others I might have found myself in. The university had accepted me as a professor, but a professor without a college is a rare and probably disconsolate figure, and I needed to attach myself. Up till then, as explained above, I had worked outside Oxbridge and knew rather little about it or its colleges – I had been there neither as an undergraduate nor as a teacher. There were other potential disqualifications: I was a grammar school boy making a belated appearance on this very different scene at the possibly inflexible age of fifty-four, and there was no particular reason why people should want me as a colleague, especially as at that date professors were not permitted to teach undergraduates, which is, after all, the main business of a college. Moreover there was some kind of quota system which allowed even colleges that might want them only a limited number of such appointments.

I discovered, however, that such obstacles can be got round, and with help from a former Provost of King's, Noel Annan, and the regnant Provost, Edmund Leach, I was accepted at King's and eventually honoured with an Honorary Fellowship, so that my connection with King's, and so (more tenuously) with E.M. Forster now extends to thirty-five years. Hence my 'sentimental' choice of topic for the lectures: it seemed almost inevitable that the chance to say something about this entirely fortuitous and one-sided relationship should be celebrated by Clark Lectures dedicated to the study of a celebrated Clark Lecturer.

Not that I intended, or could have achieved, unstinted eulogy. The first part of this little book pays some attention to all of Forster's novels, so far as the limitations of the lecture form allowed, and is only occasionally censorious. But in the second part, which takes the form of what I have called a *causerie*, Forster is reduced in size, placed in a wider context, and occasionally scolded for not being altogether the kind of author I should have preferred him to be.

What I mean by *causerie* is a free, rambling stream of more or less directly relevant comment, not organized on one basic principle of reading, like Sainte-Beuve's intense biographical stare, but aspiring more simply to what the *Oxford Dictionary* defines as 'informal talk or discussion, esp. on literary topics' – having a remote kinship with the loosely linked gossip column; or a series of discussions animated by shared interests and always having, somewhere near their centre, the enigmatic figure of Forster.

Acknowledgements

I will remember, though they may not, the exceptional kindness shown me by Professor Adrian Poole and Professor Boyd Hilton, both of Trinity College, at a critical moment during my lectures. Later I was deeply indebted, as many times before, to the editorial skill and taste of Elisabeth Sifton at Farrar, Straus and Giroux. And there were further such contributions from Bea Hemming of Weidenfeld & Nicolson. Professor Heather Glen and Ursula Owen read and did much more than I deserved to improve the book.

PART ONE

1 Aspects of Aspects

It is eighty years since E.M. Forster gave the Clark Lectures. His series was a great success, but not with everybody; Dr F.R. Leavis sat through all eight – audiences and lecturers had real stamina in those days – and recalled that he was 'astonished at the intellectual nullity that characterized them'. The only explanation for their 'gruesome success', he went on, was that the audience consisted largely of 'sillier dons and their wives'. As he was responsible for the teaching of English at Girton and Newnham, he claimed he was well placed to judge the damage caused among susceptible women students by the book in which the lectures were later published. It seems that even before they arrived in Cambridge their schoolmistresses had convinced them of Forster's importance as a critical theorist, especially as it was demonstrated, much to Dr Leavis's annoyance, by his differentiation of flat and round characters.

There was notoriously little love lost between Leavis, future editor of the severe quarterly *Scrutiny*, and members of the King's College–Bloomsbury coterie – the Woolfs, John Maynard Keynes, Lytton Strachey, Roger Fry, and so on – to which Forster belonged. Unlike Leavis, he was not a don but an independent writer, professing a highminded hedonism to which the highminded puritan Leavis might have been expected to be bleakly hostile. Yet they had more in common than appeared. Leavis's more formal and considered opinion of Forster was expressed in an essay published first in *Scrutiny* in 1938 and later in *The Common Pursuit* (1952). This essay is an exasperated tribute to the 'oddly limited and uncertain quality of [Forster's] distinction – his real and very fine distinction'. Without saying very much in detail about the novels, which he accuses of 'a curious lack of grasp', Dr Leavis congratulates Forster on the 'poise' of his art, which nevertheless 'has something equivocal in it'; his 'felicities ... involve limitations'. And he finds, in the earlier novels particularly, a characteristic 'spinsterly touch'. (This epithet is used again in the essay.) He goes on to make the necessary comparisons and limiting judgements: compared with Henry James Forster is 'only too unmistakably minor'. *Howards End* has an inherent weakness, a sentimentality, a lack of contact with the real (for instance, in the treatment of Leonard Bast). Leavis's dislike of the liberal culture of Bloomsbury entails some severity of judgement even on *A Passage to India*. But the essay ends, rather unexpectedly, with a 'parting salute': a recommendation that 'Forster's is a name that, in these days we should peculiarly honour'.

A good deal of what has been written on Forster has this shape: he irritates readers who nevertheless feel obliged, in the end, to do him honour. I think that's right, and will pay the debt of honour without ceding my right to some bouts of irritation. I do believe that Forster was an artist of peculiar distinction; excellent books have been written to prove it. But I also believe that there are reasons for dissentient judgements and some of these I shall try to express. To do so may, in the end, be a way of paying more tribute, for the causes of irritation may well be closely related to the causes of admiration.

I haven't, given my prescribed scope, been able to treat of any of the novels at any length, hoping only that some parts of them, lit from unfamiliar angles, may strike even readers learned in Forster as new and valuable. This first chapter is more panoramic than the others, the viewing point being *Aspects of the Novel*. In the second I'll be concentrating on Forster and music (Benjamin Britten called him the most musical of our novelists, and the point will stand looking at). In the third my eye is mostly though not exclusively on *A Passage to India*, the book I believe without reservation or equivocation to be his greatest.

Forster regarded himself as an artist. Unpublished or uncollected material is still turning up in impressive quantities, and a fairly large proportion of it consists of criticism of one kind or another, but he believed that criticism was of almost no use to art and artists. His own art was fiction, but he said firmly, in a broadcast of 1944, that 'the novel ... has not any rules and there is no such thing as the art of fiction'. This remark needs qualifying: he was proud of his own work as an artist. He understood what Virginia Woolf was trying to do and knew that she also was an artist, though with a 'method' different from his own. As to criticism, he not only wrote piles of it, mostly in the form of reviews, short essays and occasional lectures or memoirs read to friends, but was capable of dropping his usual persona, the mild, intelligent, undemanding conversationalist, and of treating unworthy opposites with chilling contempt. Oswald Mosley, Edward VII and his biographer Sidney Lee are scorned, though with less severity than Hilaire Belloc and Gauguin and John Middleton Murry and Christian missionaries. Christabel Pankhurst suffers the kind of justice she would have preferred to ignore ('very able, very clever, and very unpleasant', thought Forster, though he 'agreed with most of her remarks'). A.E. Housman, for whose poems he had a deep affection, he made unsuccessful attempts to cultivate – Housman lived for many years in Trinity, five minutes away from King's College – but he had no luck; he neatly summed up the great man's 'combination of unamiability and creative power'. Of a novel by the French statesman Georges Clemenceau – whose prowess as a novelist may have been great in the immediate post-war years though, I suppose, no longer – he offered a test of lifelessness: 'Pinch the book where you will, and it does not move.'

With Henry James the quarrel was more polite but also more important. Forster respected James, but judging by the number of occasions on which he expressed his disappointment with James's work his heart wasn't really in it. He could bear some of James's earlier work but he drew the line at *What Maisie Knew* ('I haven't *quite* got through her yet, but I think I shall: she is my very limit – beyond her lies *The Golden Bowl*, *The Ambassadors* and similar impossibilities') and he regarded *The Sense of the Past* as the only tolerable specimen of late James. In short, he might be described as habitually unreceptive to James. When he was twenty he read *Portrait of a Lady* and commented, 'it is very wonderful, but there's something wrong with him or me: he is not George Meredith' (Meredith was venerated at the time, though rejected later). When he visited James at Rye the great man mistook him for somebody else – for G.E. Moore as it happened – which may or may not have softened the blow.

What repelled him in James was the lack, as Forster saw it, of solidity and of character, and the preoccupation with what James took to be the art of fiction, with 'pattern', what James would call 'the doing' – a fanatical attachment to the treatment of the subject rather than to the material Forster regarded as the basic novelistic substance, the rendering of bourgeois life. Forster did not disapprove of experiment – one could argue that, in their ways, his own novels are all experimental – but he found the Jamesian experiments bloodless and without savour. 'What did he mean by art? Well, something that doesn't interest us much now, and that's why he's so neglected.' This judgement was made in 1931, but catches Forster's permanent discontent with James. 'He seems to me our only perfect novelist, but alas, it isn't a very enthralling type of perfection.' So with Virginia Woolf: he admired her innovations but strongly defended his own practice against hers. We need to remember that although his writings on fiction were voluminous they were also, for the most part, occasional, and he was under no obligation to provide systematic comment on his contemporaries. Still, it does seem odd that he has little or nothing of interest to say about many of them, including his near contemporary Ford Madox Ford, who was not only a very good novelist but a fertile theorist, respected by the avant-garde. Forster didn't have much interest in the avant-garde as such, though on occasion he praised the work of individuals associated with it.

But the main opponent, the acknowledged master who departed so wilfully from the tradition as he believed it should be properly understood, was James. Given that he represented an attitude to fiction more or less diametrically opposite to Forster's, he provided a necessary target in *Aspects*, and the work that had to suffer the lecturer's quietly charitable dissection was one of the 'impossibles', *The Ambassadors*. Forster gave it more attention than any other novel, except possibly Gide's *Les Faux-Monnayeurs*, though the intention in that case also was hostile.

Part of the case against James in *Aspects* is made by allusion to a painful and famous disagreement between James and H.G. Wells. This quiet but momentous quarrel had its origin in an article James wrote in the *Times Literary Supplement* in 1914 on the younger generation of novelists. In 'The New Novel', he surveyed at some length the contemporary state of fiction (though without allusion to Forster) and lamented the defective art of a great many industrious practitioners. His principal targets were Arnold Bennett and H.G. Wells. These were writers he could not dismiss out of hand, but he complained that neither was interested in what he liked to call the 'doing'.

Objecting to James's remarks on his work and Arnold Bennett's, Wells attacked James in *Boon* (1915), a book that was more a collection of squibs than a novel. He accused James of creating lifeless characters and sacrificing everything to the demands of artistic unity. 'The thing his novel is *about*,' said Wells, 'is always there. It is like a church lit but without a congregation to distract you, with every light and line focused on the high altar. And on the altar, very reverently placed, intensely there, is a dead kitten, an egg-shell, a bit of string.'

James wrote Wells what in the circumstances was a friendly letter. He had remarked in his essay on what he called the absence of 'interest' in Wells and Bennett, and now spoke for his own interest: 'I hold that interest may be, must be, exquisitely made and created, and that if we don't make it, we who undertake to, nobody & nothing will make it for us.' Wells replied that he had a natural horror of 'dignity, finish and perfection'. He felt that James's contrary views had too much influence, and choosing to be a journalist rather than an artist, he thought it right to challenge James's attitude and maintain his own kind of 'interest'. James's response, wounded but courteous, ends with a famous declaration: 'It is art that *makes* life, makes interest, makes importance ... and I know of no substitute whatever for the force and beauty of the process.'

In *Aspects of the Novel* Forster seems quite pleased to see James ridiculed, and firmly awards the judgement to Wells – a disquieting conclusion in view of the philistinism of Wells's satire and the studied insolence of his replies to letters in which James, having allowed himself a mild criticism of his friend's manners, nevertheless took the trouble to explain his position, and to convey his inevitable decision to renounce any attempt to understand Wells's.

Having enjoyed the comedy of James's discomfiture, Forster declares that his quarrel with Wells has, nevertheless, 'literary importance'. The question immediately at issue is that of the rigid pattern; the hour-glass shape of *The Ambassadors* is achieved at the cost of 'life'. Wells had said that 'life should be given the preference and must not be whittled or distended for a pattern's sake', and Forster agrees. To James this is heresy. Bennett's novel *Clayhanger*, he had memorably remarked, is 'a monument exactly not to an idea, a pursued and captured meaning, or in short, *to* anything whatever, but just simply *of* the quarried and gathered material it happens to contain, the stones and bricks and rubble and cement and promiscuous constituents of every sort that have been heaped in it'. As for Wells, his procedures were tantamount to his turning 'out his mind and its contents upon us by any free familiar gesture and as from a high window forever open'. James's case against both novelists he summed up thus: 'Yes, yes – but is this *all*? These are the circumstances of the interest – we see, we see – but where is the interest itself, where and what is its centre . . . ?'

As it happens, the gifted Bennett was capable of the kind of novel that James might have approved but *Riceyman Steps* came too late for him to comment. (That duty was undertaken by Virginia Woolf, whose comments on *Riceyman Steps* are remarkably obtuse.) Bennett was capable, and knew himself to be capable, of Jamesian refinements. But he preferred to be read by the multitude, and so did Wells. The differences between, say, *The Golden Bowl* and anything Wells would have wanted to write are clear enough. As Wells expressed it, 'James begins by taking it for granted that a novel is a work of art that must be judged by its oneness. Someone gave him that idea in the beginning of things and he has never found it out'. For Wells it was a question of choosing between doing art and doing life. But for James doing art *was* doing life. He said so in the beautiful letter to Wells that ended their argument.

'My own prejudices are with Wells,' wrote Forster, who believed you could do anything with a novel, use any technical move to 'bounce' the reader, as he put it, so long as you got away with it. But what he wished to get away with *was* a form of the art that makes life and importance, that was, to recall his own pronouncement, 'the one orderly product our muddling race has produced'. In short he was on the side of James, but he allowed his distaste for the pattern, and the prose, and the sacrifice of realistic character to persuade him, in this instance, to disparage the force and beauty of James's art.

Forster's first four novels were written in the same years – the first decade of the twentieth century – as James's Prefaces to the New York edition of his novels. One might have expected the youthful Forster, himself searching for original ways to treat traditional forms, to be impressed by these remarkable exercises, which had such a powerful influence on later writers and critics. For example, re-reading *What Maisie Knew* elicited from the fluent master a full account of the genesis and maturing of his story, with special reference to the technical difficulty of making the little girl the central consciousness of the narrative. Maisie cannot be expected to possess a full understanding of her parents' divorce and subsequent behaviour ('the infant mind would at the best leave great gaps and voids'). But it is exactly here that James sees the possibilities that interest him; he likes, he says, to glory in the gap – in this case the gap between what Maisie's parents are up to and what she, with her limited knowledge and experience, can make of it; and he conceives it to be the business of art to give the reader a full sense of the affair on the information acquired from this imperfect source. He is pleased with the result: 'nothing could be more "done", I think, in the light of its happiest intention'.

I don't know whether Forster read or even glanced at the Prefaces, but it is safe to surmise that any admiration he felt for them would have been in this case quite severely qualified. His friend Percy Lubbock in his unexciting treatise *The Craft of Fiction* was fervently on the side of James, maintaining that a novel must have but one character entitled to a point of view; in *The Ambassadors* (the very book Forster chose to make his disapproval plain) that character was Strether. Forster was not impressed; James was devoted to his 'aesthetic duty', he wrote, 'but at what sacrifice! ... Most of human life has to disappear before he can do us a novel.' The characters are 'deformed', sacrificed to James's ideal. Had he set himself to develop a story of this kind, Forster would have favoured a much less oblique approach; he affirmed the author's right to express his opinions, his right, if he chose, to explain to the reader directly how, in his view, the matter appeared when looked at in its relation not to Strether or Maisie but to such other characters as he chose to use, or simply to the universe.

Observations on the universe, on love, and friendship and many other important matters occur boldly and frequently in Forster's novels. It may be allowed that in *Howards End* the characters are represented as free individuals, with minds of their own, but the book contains a strikingly large amount of authorial reflection, wise sayings about love, class and culture, panic and emptiness, prose and passion, connecting and not connecting, straightforward announcements of the Forsterian way of looking at the human condition. In *A Passage to India* there are moments that must have been intended to shock the Jamesian purist by addressing the 'dear reader', and, in the many ways open to him, explaining or suggesting how he felt about his characters (though he claimed they always kept their freedom) and – he doesn't avoid the word – the universe. If Forster had tackled a situation like Maisie's, it would not have been Maisie's perception of it that more or less exclusively occupied his interest.

The differences between the two novelists may be expressed succinctly by comparing James and Forster on Tolstoy. To Forster *War and Peace* was the greatest of all novels; to James it was something of a disaster: 'what do such large loose baggy monsters, with their queer elements of the accidental and the arbitrary, artistically *mean*?' Worse still, 'his example for others is dire'. And yet, as we shall see, Forster, so firm in dismissing James on the art of the novel and even denying that such a thing existed, claimed to be an artist whose medium was the novel; and he justified the claim. What he was not prepared to do was to regard the novelist's art as a struggle with problems like those James loved to set himself; the writing of fiction was difficult enough without what he saw as arbitrary and artificial handicaps, such as consigning the narrative to one particular and necessarily defective consciousness.

Since about 1969 the study of narrative, taking forms undreamed of by Forster, has been called 'narratology'. It is impossible not to admire the ingenuity of such major narratologists as Roland Barthes and Gérard Genette, for instance. In this context we should observe that the only passage in Forster's *Aspects* as famous as the one about flat and round characters is the one that establishes a distinction between story and plot. He makes it sound simple. Time and the narratologists have shown that it is not. The distinction between the text and the story it contains – between *fabula* and *sujet*, as the Russian and Czech Formalists expressed it, between *récit* (or *histoire*) and *discourse* (or *sujet*) – has been subjected to extraordinary refinements, with particular reference to the distortions of the chronological order of events as they may be inferred to occur in the *fabula*.

In a sense there is nothing very arcane about this. We take it as natural that story-tellers should sometimes go back and recount events that significantly lead up to the situation they are describing. If – to take an example once famous in a hundred graduate classrooms – you begin a novel with the sentence *La marquise sortit à cinq heures* (as Claude Mauriac did, in 1961, challenging Paul Valéry's assertion that one couldn't do anything with such a banality), you can be sure that later on there will be some explanation of what has induced her to do so, and perhaps some explanation of why the order of the *fabula* is violated by the *récit*'s rush *in medias res*. After all, Homer and Virgil made the practice canonical. Or perhaps two related sequences of events are to be represented as occurring simultaneously: hence 'meanwhile, back at the ranch ...', for instance, where we return to an earlier point in the story and need a signal to warn us of the chronological disturbance. But Genette, whose examples are mostly drawn from Proust, and are evidence of a higher degree of literary intelligence than is quite general, refines these insights and assumptions, and provides elegant labels for certain manoeuvres we had probably not imagined they needed. So what we called 'flashbacks' are now anachronies, and so are 'flashforwards'. Discordances between the order of story and that of the narrative can be methodically regulated, though ordinary readers may not see the need, understanding from their nursery years that 'Some months earlier' can introduce events which occur earlier in the story but later in the narrative, or vice versa. But the narratologist will distinguish analepses as either homodiegetic or heterodiegetic, according to the status or otherwise of the story affected by the analeptic intrusion.

Narratologists do not mind that the ever-increasing refinement of their instruments may be criticized as affectedly neologistic and cumbersome; they have what Gerald Prince, a narratologist himself, calls an 'infatuation with science' even when they are talking about the process of story-telling, something understood by 'every human society known to history'. The novelist Christine Brooke-Rose, in an essay resigning her own *deuxième carrière* as a narratologist, described narratology as 'immensely useful. But in the end, it couldn't cope with narrative and its complexities, except at the price of becoming a separate theoretical discourse, rarely relevant to the narrative discussed, *when discussed*.' And there certainly are people who treat narratology as a theoretical discourse to be considered in isolation from the texts that provide its origin. Often, as Gerald Prince suggests, though not always, it offers a complicated 'scientific' account of reading practices that are already second nature to almost all readers. Its use may be greater when the story under consideration is recounted in a manner meant to draw attention to deviations of point of view, of chronological progression and so on. Readers of William Faulkner's novels know how such practices can darken the sense of the narrative; Ford Madox Ford also uses them, less darkly. Other writers may employ the same devices for comic effect or to set interpretative puzzles for skilful readers; and they may do so without making life too difficult for readers who want the story to be reasonably clear in the telling.

Let me offer an example of some feats of reading that we

all do very easily, but which could be made to be or to seem arcane if one were infatuated by science. Try to narratologize Muriel Spark's *The Prime of Miss Jean Brodie*. Miss Brodie's girls, the Brodie 'set', are sixteen years old at the outset of the novel and have been a set since they were twelve. The date is now 1936. It is six years since Brodie told the girls she intended to make them the *crème de la crème*. Brodie is under threat from colleagues who disapprove of her teaching methods, but she still maintains that her prime has begun. One girl, Sandy, watches events with her treacherous little piggy eyes ('it was astonishing that anyone could trust' her), and we watch those events as the untrustworthy Sandy observes and reports them at various ages and in various amorous and religious situations. In 1930 the girls are ten. We have reached page 13 when we learn that Mary MacGregor is stupid, and on page 15 she dies in a hotel fire at the age of twenty-four, date presumably 1944, courtesy of an act of forward analepsis or prolepsis. Mary's death is again displaced when her future death in the hotel fire, still years into the future, is prefigured by the account of her terror of fire in the science room in 1931, on page 25, when she is eleven. Important discussions about sex take place between Sandy and Jenny, far into the simple chronological future; and Jenny, after sixteen years of marriage, experiences a moment of love. Eunice, aged forty-four in the narration, recalls doing the splits at sixteen, her age in the story. We are told, ahead of time, that Miss Brodie dies 'just after the war' (in 1945), but this information is proffered before we learn of the momentous walk she took with her girls through the poorest parts of Edinburgh, the parts inhabited by the people the Scots call 'the Idle'– as reported on page 30. Later, on page 56, we find out that she had retired 'before time' and that she died of 'an internal growth' at fifty-six. She had survived to lament Sandy's entering a convent. On page 34 we learn that Sandy, after another lapse of years, is a famous writer, now named Sister Helena of the Transfiguration.

And so on. I can manage only a poor idea of the chronological manipulations. What we know about Sandy, and, to a lesser extent, the other girls, we cannot derive from a straightforward narrative, but must take the fragments when they occur and build our own picture, continually altered by the shifting context. The point is that Spark has taken further the ability of narrative to submit to timeshifts which result in your reading the denouement of the story before it is conventionally launched and developed. She has lots of these timeshifts, and though they may surprise the reader, they are well within his or her inherited capacity to deal with narrative – not only because much day-to-day story-telling permits discontinuities that present no difficulty to interlocutors, but because the action of narrative resembles the action of memory and exercises it. Little clues, repetitive phrases and incidents make one alert to the possibility that a narrative may conceal the significance of reported events, saving it for later discovery and fulfilment; events and the words that report them, decorously related near the end of the story, may suddenly illuminate earlier reticences not at first recognizable as such. This may sound difficult, but we do it easily, though experiencing many mild and agreeable surprises. It is true that most novels don't do this 'giving things away', not at any rate on the scale and with the wantonness of Mrs Spark's book; they are merely complying with the norm that makes possible her virtuoso variations.

What benefits accrue from all this analepsis? What would be lost if the story was told consecutively – 'and then and then and then ...'? The American novelist Theodore Dreiser, reviewing Ford Madox Ford's *The Good Soldier*, said that if he'd had occasion to advise Ford he would have told him to begin at the beginning 'so that the story continued in a more or less direct line'. What a difference that would have made! Dreiser wanted to take away the very devices of which Ford was proudest, those misleading collocations of report, those dangerous liaisons of events as well as of characters, that were meant to give his novel the historical resonance he was trying for; Ford thought of the story as something to be transformed, presented as an 'affair', as he put it, in the interest of art – seeking the imprimatur of James, not Forster.

Much the same may be said of Spark's slighter novel. It has strong unelaborated underplots: political – Miss Brodie's flirtations with fascism; religious – the latent distorted Calvinism of Brodie's 'electing herself to grace'; her determination to pass on her culture and status as one of the many thousands of women deprived by the Great War of the prospect of marriage (to remind us, a male master in her school has lost an arm).

I have not even tried to explain why this novella is so funny and so intelligently packed and patterned; only describing as best I could the constant interference with the *sujet*, *histoire* or whatever, particularly in the matter of chronological telling. The result could be made to sound chaotic. Yet no reader I know of has ever complained of difficulty in following this story. The dislocations may sometimes seem justified, sometimes wanton, virtuoso displays; but they are intelligible extensions of practices familiar from thousands of stories; and under this *sujet* the scope of reference is greatly increased. A good reader will apprehend what may seem remote from the story, deep and possibly disturbing political and religious resonances.

Forster liked to have something he called religion in his novels, and James's not having any was part of Forster's indictment against him. Forster could not have complained that Spark was deficient in the supernatural, and he believed the comic element in fiction to be important and endangered, but he might still have thought Spark's liberties over the top; they do fail to provide a simple account of causality, which is something he tried to get into *Aspects of the Novel*. Not that Spark's novel has no plot but, rather, that she arbitrarily and with great skill fragments the story's chronology, making the plot seem arbitrarily fragmented. Yet as a resourceful story-teller himself Forster would probably have enjoyed the assurance of the telling, perhaps adding a warning that these things should not be overdone, that story can be stifled by plot, *fabula* by *récit*.

On such matters he may indeed have felt he had said enough in *Aspects of the Novel*, and said it simply and memorably, perhaps too memorably – to the relief of Girton and Newnham and the disgust of Downing. The book was a big success, though of a genre in which Forster might not have expected success. And that is good cause for congratulation: it was good that he, so sceptical about the value of all criticism, should test the opinion as a practitioner. Yet it remains possible to complain that in a book on such a subject he ought, perhaps, to have looked about him rather more, and found something more to say about certain works by his contemporaries, especially those who made formal experiments and believed they had found new and better ways of telling the truth in fiction.

Forster did, of course, tackle the question of novel theory in his remarks on James and Lubbock. He thought that people who advertised the power of their methods ended by valuing the method above the work under consideration. Anyway the large library of narratology that we now have wasn't available to him. In 1928 there were many fewer specialist theoretical studies at hand, and what there were he disliked. There was

Lubbock's *The Craft of Fiction* (1921), but Lubbock, a fellow Kingsman, had been his boss in Egypt, which may be why Forster concealed his distaste for a work that boasted an irritatingly reverent and exclusive focus on Henry James. Forster's review of Clayton Hamilton's *Materials and Methods of Fiction* (1919) was contemptuous; he particularly disliked its treatment of that central Jamesian topic, point of view, and he remembered the book disparagingly in the introductory chapter of *Aspects*.

Edwin Muir's *Structure of the Novel* (1928) came just too late for Forster to address in his lectures, and indeed the book shows an acquaintance with them. Muir shared Forster's enthusiasm for Proust, saying that Proust had written a novel resembling Gide's *Les Faux-Monnayeurs* in that it was a novel about a novelist writing a novel. This is of course true; as Genette remarked, you can tell the story of *À la recherche* in four words, 'Marcel becomes a writer', but that was not the aspect of Proust that appealed to Forster. (I'll try later to say what that was.) More to the Forsterian point, Muir also notes that Proust 'takes any and every way, moves backwards and forwards as he likes, led not by the story but by the psychological movement behind it'.

However, they agreed in not much liking *Ulysses*. Muir thought it lacked 'causality' and that the Homeric scaffolding was a failure and couldn't prevent the book from being 'formless'. Virginia Woolf also disliked it. These reactions to *Ulysses* reinforce one's sense that many of the best novelists of the period, Forster included, quite urgently wanted innovation and would have surely welcomed it if it had turned up; yet when it did – as in James and Ford and Lawrence and Joyce, for example – it was met with suspicion. Conrad, said Virginia Woolf, remained an exotic, 'not so much an influence as an idol, honoured and admired but aloof and apart'. Eyes turned instead to the Russian novels as they appeared in French translations or in the English translations of Constance Garnett. Flaubert and Maupassant were accepted as models, along with Turgenev. Forster, like others who felt that the needed change could not come from English writers, welcomed Proust's *À la recherche du temps perdu* with insight and sincerity when the first parts of that novel began to appear in English in the 1920s. He complained, even as he was working on *A Passage to India*, that he was 'bored by the tiresomeness and conventionalities of fiction-form' ... 'some change must be made'. That thought was now strongly associated with Proust. There was to be no revolutionary change in Forster's style, but in subtle ways Proust had his effect.

The demand for a new style of novel – for the rejection of the nineteenth-century model – was probably related to the rapid technological developments in other spheres. This was the age of the Dreadnought, the motor car was multiplying, mass production was under way. Technology was most unlikely to make a world Forster wanted – a world in which novel writing could still be practised as a cottage industry.

There were experimental writers (Muir named three as innovators of consequence: Woolf, Joyce and Aldous Huxley), but how to talk about them was a bit of a puzzle; there seemed to be no vocabulary. James made up vocabularies as he went along, but others were less fluent. The modern way of talking about these matters can be dated to 1961 with Wayne Booth's *The Rhetoric of Fiction*, a really impressive work; the second edition (1983) shows how fast this once newish topic moved forward and attracted academic attention. Booth has much to say about point of view, but, genially moralistic, he declines to deprive the author, or his lay figure the Implied Author, of responsibility for the moral implications of the narrative. His book dominated discussion on this subject until we discovered the work of the French rhetoricians and, through them, the Czech and Russian Formalists, with results I have already touched on.

But, as I say, Forster would not have cared for these novelties. They had no place in liberal society as he understood it. He belonged to a stubborn English tradition that shies away from Theory: 'If we wheel up aesthetic theory,' he said in a Harvard lecture delivered in 1947, 'The Raison d'être of Criticism in the Arts', 'and apply it with its measuring rods and pliers and forceps, its callipers and catheters [to a work of art] we are visited at once by a sense of the grotesque. It doesn't work; two universes have not even collided, they have been juxtaposed.' But the new methods and theories prevailed, at any rate in the universities; the theory of narrative produced dozens of books and obsessed hundreds of academics. A whole academic generation not only challenged the assumptions of the older dons but created a bracing, if possibly illusory impression that we now had a 'science of literature' with narratology as an important department. Not to be a technologist was now to be not merely a dilettante but a violator of the new institutional order.

I shall say no more about this new and impressive machinery except that, as in a modern kitchen, the equipment can win more attention than the food. Forster's attitude to these innovations would probably have resembled his view of motor cars in *Howards End* – destructive, smelly and intrusive, and associated with the kind of people he felt little need to know. Moreover there was a question concerning the value of the novels on which the new science went to work; being a science, narratology is value-free; one could do clever things with the rods and pliers and catheters to any piece of fiction that came along. Roland Barthes notoriously analysed the James Bond novels. It was the machinery that occupied one's attention. As

Brooke-Rose remarked, narratology was self-reflexive in the best post-modern way. In that way it has its interest, but Forster can be excused from showing the slightest interest in the subject.

There is, however, a charge more difficult to evade. *Aspects of the Novel* has remarkably little to say about Forster's contemporaries. It is true that Wells and James, of course, and also Gide, Max Beerbohm, Arnold Bennett, Samuel Butler, Galsworthy, David Garnett, Thomas Hardy, Robert Hitchens, W.H. Hudson, Lubbock and H. de Vere Stacpoole are mentioned, along with Forster's close friend G.L. Dickinson. Of another friend, Virginia Woolf, he has very little to say, merely a glancing though favourable allusion. While he was writing *Aspects*, she published *To the Lighthouse*, a work he admired and found 'exciting in its formal innovations', but he did not discuss either this novel or any of its predecessors in his lectures. In a letter she wrote after reading *Aspects of the Novel*, Woolf said that if she were writing a book about fiction she would 'hunt a little'. That may be fair comment. Forster was a reader, and he even took Woolf's advice, up to a point, while preparing for these lectures, but although contemporaries are often mentioned in his Commonplace Book and in essays and reviews, he evidently chose not to praise or blame them in his lectures, unless they won attention by their eminence, like James, Gide and Proust.

Among other contemporaries of Forster were novelists who took a keen protonarratological interest in developing new ways of relating *fabula* and *sujet*, of avoiding a straightforward representation of causality as the mark of their difference, desiring to alter the emphasis, to light scenes in a way that could not be achieved with ordinary ideas of chronological order, point of view or cause and effect. Forster says quite expressly that 'we do not mind the shifting of our viewpoint' – we accept it without fuss in *Bleak House*, for example, in which the omniscient narrator of the opening hands over to Esther Summerson – but he draws the line at Gide's *Les Faux-Monnayeurs*, a novel greatly admired in his day, including as it does various points of view and a character who is writing a book called *Les Faux-Monnayeurs*. It also contains discussions of the art of the novel. Gide, he writes, is 'a little more solemn than an author should be about the whole caboodle'. What has Forster to say about *Ulysses*? 'Does it come off? Not quite.' He glances at Gertrude Stein: she tried to banish the clock from the novel; it can't be done.

What might he have said about Ford Madox Ford's *The Good Soldier*? As I've suggested, one would have expected Forster to know something about Ford (they had met; Forster described him as 'fly-blown'), but he does not mention Ford in *Aspects* (there are a few words from a newspaper article on Ford's death and reputation: nothing of substance), perhaps because of Ford's well-known close attachments to Conrad and James. Ford was offended by Forster's treatment of Gide in *Aspects*; he thought Forster's casual dismissal of Gide's experiment was typically British – but Ford was also British, though Francophile, and himself wrote a good deal about many aspects of the novel.

One thing Ford said was that the composition of a novel must involve not the representation of a chronological series of events but 'the exhaustion of aspects', and one way to exhaust them required the use of Conradian time-shifts, the arrangement of climaxes that lead, not necessarily in chronological order, to the end of a story. The actual end of a story, considered in relation to the chronologically displaced 'effects' throughout, may be the least interesting thing about it. But a novel should conclude by revealing 'once and for all, in the last sentence or the penultimate ... the psychological significance of the whole' as revealed by the disparately presented 'aspects'. Thus there should be throughout not a sequence of 'and thens' but a 'progression of effects' conspiring to this end. Along the way the reader may face deliberate deceptions in both the English and French meanings of the word, both mis-reported events and disappointments. Ford accepted James's statement that there was a need to establish 'a baffled relation between the subject matter and its emergence' – something rather more taxing than the normal business of finding one's bearings in the opening pages – and he wrote at least one novel that obeys most of his rules, rules that have seemed good to some good novelists, as well as to some critics, for almost a century.

That is partly why the history of the twentieth-century novel is often written in terms of books that Forster disparaged or neglected to mention. What he would have made of William Faulkner I can't conjecture; in *The Sound and the Fury* (1929) the events of the story are described by four different characters, the first of them an idiot who lacks any idea of time; there is certainly no clock in his section, any more than there is in Gertrude Stein. Even less likely to please Forster, the French *nouveau roman* claimed realism but defied ordinary notions of character and causality, and it was backed by Alain Robbe-Grillet's own theoretical programme and the blessing of Barthes.

Still, Forster really ought to have known and said something about Ford's *The Good Soldier*. The novel depends heavily upon an 'unreliable narrator' – a dull, impotent, easily deceived man who claims to be telling 'the saddest story I have ever heard', when he is himself at the very centre of the story, betrayed by his wife and his friends, involved in pregnant episodes which he simply does not understand and which can sometimes induce in the reader a bewilderment almost as deep as his own. Ford is making a joke about point-of-view: in his novel the possessor of it doesn't even know he has it. Chronological dislocations abound; the order of the *histoire* or fable is sacrificed to the interests of the *sujet*, with a strangeness of effect like that which Conrad had sometimes sought, but exceeding those of *Nostromo*. When Ford reviewed *Aspects of the Novel* he found it very unsatisfactory; his own aspects, quite copiously recorded elsewhere, are of a different kind and quality altogether.

On one view, there is a lot wrong with *The Good Soldier*, places where, under scrupulous examination, the story and the treatment don't exactly match up. In another sense this doesn't matter, since the man who is telling the story doesn't understand it himself, and the mistakes can all be attributed to him, or called a challenge to the reader's vigilance. This is true even if we admit that Ford was obsessed by dates; he wanted every critical action of the story to take place on August 4 (which happened to be the date when the First World War began). The scheme is implausible and impractical and he cannot manage it. He regarded that date as the one on which European civilization came to an end – a disaster comparable, in his view, to the Reformation, which figures in one of the darkest, strangest, and apparently least consequential passages of his book. Ford said he wanted to make the reader's mind pass 'perpetually backwards and forwards between the apparent aspect of things and the essentials of life' – a programme Forster might not have rejected, though he would probably have preferred to fulfil it without breaking up the story into discontinuous pieces.

One can say, I think, that Ford and Forster deserve equal praise for the brilliance of their opening chapters in *The Good Soldier* and *A Passage to India*; here, at least, are displays of technique virtually impossible to match, and yet they are very different – Ford all crafty concealments and potential misunderstandings, Forster establishing in one beautifully crafted sentence the great scope of his theme.

I wish Forster had written about Ford's book, but I suspect he would have given it much the same treatment as he handed out to James and Gide. That thought gives us reason to guess that we at least know what aspects of the novel the author of *Aspects of the Novel* would close his door to. That doesn't mean we have discovered what sort of writing Forster would be sure to welcome. Could we have guessed, for instance, that Proust would be let in? Proust, whose disregard for straightforward chronological reporting, his 'moving backward and forward as he likes', and over such an immense area, could well have seemed inept or wilful? Yet Forster not merely admired *À la recherche du temps perdu* but described it as the second best novel after *War and Peace*.

What, then, is to be said by way of summing up *Aspects*? I have suggested that its scope is limited, but Forster might well have replied by pointing out that he was happy to have learned his basic craft from Jane Austen rather than James or Conrad. He maintained that the way to write novels was not to have a complex programme but in each case to do whatever was justified by results.

The book, though short, is curiously dilute; Forster had no intention of boring his audience. If he could not please Dr Leavis he could be happy that A.E. Housman was among his auditors; he paid him the graceful compliment of an unheralded quotation, as if to say that his other hearers ought also to recognize the lines from his poem 'Eight O'Clock' ('the very moment of doom, when "the clock collected in the tower its strength and struck"'). He discusses with civilized humour the questions of story and plot, allows for the action of memory on the order of events, and gets close to describing plot in terms that Ford could have accepted: 'something which is measured not by minutes or hours, but by intensity, so that when we look at our past it does not stretch back evenly but piles up into a few notable pinnacles' – which may, in the end, if desired, be described as the products of Genettian homodiegetic analepsis.

Later I shall talk a bit about Forster's interest in *greatness*. Lionel Trilling remarked on his 'refusal to be great', and this shrewd observation is quoted by almost everybody who writes about Forster. But in fact greatness interested Forster greatly, and he is not joking when he stands some English novels, however rich and accomplished, in the colonnades of *War and Peace* or the vaults of *The Brothers Karamazov* and cuts them down to size. And yet even English novels, he thinks, can 'give us the illusion of perspicacity and power'. Forster understands that illusion and will feed it himself. He does not often allude to his own practice, but the chapter called 'Pattern and Rhythm', the most original and interesting in *Aspects of the Novel*, obliquely does so, and I shall return to it.

In his book on Forster (the first to be devoted to him), Lionel Trilling writes of 'the sudden strictures of judgement which are the best stuff of Forster's social imagination' – a perceptive comment on an aspect of Forster's novels I have so far neglected. Trilling also remarks on a less tangible, less explicit quality, to be found notably in *A Passage to India*: what he calls the 'web of reverberation' in that book ('No thought, no deed in this book of echoes, is ever lost'). This 'reverberation' gives the novel 'a cohesion and intricacy usually found only in music' – an observation that could be the epigraph of my next chapter.

2 Beethoven, Wagner, Vinteuil

According to Benjamin Britten, Forster was 'our most musical novelist'. It was by way of an article by Forster about the poet George Crabbe (published in *The Listener* in May 1941) that Britten came upon the idea for his first opera, *Peter Grimes*. He was so pleased that Forster liked his music that he presented him with a score of his 'Michelangelo Sonnets' and also with a gramophone, and despite the thirty-odd-year gap in their ages they became friends. When Forster went to Aldeburgh to give a lecture on Crabbe he stayed with Britten and Peter Pears and shared their musical evenings. In 1951, when Britten was asked to write an opera for the Festival of Britain, Forster collaborated with Eric Crozier on the libretto of *Billy Budd*. That enterprise required him to work closely with the composer, which he did, though not without some friction; but this first-hand experience of writing words for music must have both drawn upon and enhanced the novelist's musical interests. He was particularly proud of the monologue he wrote for Claggart, the master-at-arms, and of the way he dealt with the problem of making it conspicuously different from what was inevitably its model, Iago's 'Credo' in Verdi's *Otello*.

In a tribute to Forster on his eightieth birthday in 1959, Britten expressed admiration for the scene in *Howards End* about a performance of Beethoven's Fifth Symphony: 'it shows a most sensitive reaction to music and allows the novelist to make some perceptive observations on Beethoven'. This judgement has an authority conferred by the greatness of the speaker yet may lose a little of it to some reduction of candour arising from considerations of friendship. Britten also remarked that he had heard Forster play Beethoven piano sonatas 'with spirit'. What that means is not easy to say; Lucy Honeychurch, in *A Room With a View*, also plays with spirit but does not escape censure, though she has given what sounds like a semi-public performance at Tunbridge Wells. As an undergraduate Forster had played duets with the great Oscar Browning, which may testify to his nerve as much as to his pianism. And there may be, in Britten's remark, a touch of the great performer looking down kindly from the heights of his own virtuosity and giving marks for worthy amateur effort. However that may be, it is certain that Forster's musical interests were no mere pastimes but affected his work as a novelist.

There are, I think, only three pianists in his novels: Lucy Honeychurch, to whom I shall return; a mysterious Miss Quested who plays MacDowell, though inaudibly, in *Howards End*; and, perhaps surprisingly, Leonard Bast, also of that novel. Bast plays, but according to Forster's manuscript plays 'badly'. Before the book reached print this had developed into 'badly and vulgarly' – as usual, Forster did not allow Bast to be comfortable with the middle-class culture to which he aspired and to which Forster belonged.

There can be no doubt that Forster was familiar with a wide range of music. He certainly had a more than casual interest in the Beethoven piano sonatas. In February 1918, writing from Alexandria, he informed his friend Florence Barger that he was, at the time, playing the second movement of the Waldstein sonata, Schumann's Carnaval, some Chopin Preludes and César Franck's Prelude, Aria and Finale. (He seems to have had an enduring affection for Franck, describing his

Violin Sonata as 'most important' and his Quintet as 'the greatest human achievement of my lifetime'.) In Cambridge he also once accompanied a performance by 'the grocer's boy', 'an insufferable youth', of Iago's 'Credo' in Verdi's *Otello*, an occasion he might well have remembered when writing the part of Claggart in *Billy Budd*.

His interest in the Beethoven sonatas did not fade. Early in the Second World War he began, at the instance of his friend Charles Mauron, to write a study of them. He worked at the keyboard, resorting to records when the music became too hard. He himself notes in an essay called 'Not Listening to Music' (1939) that his own performances on the piano 'grow worse yearly', but he thinks he ought to go on playing all the same because, he says, 'they teach me a little about construction. I see what becomes of a phrase, how it is transformed or returned, sometimes bottom upward, and get some notion of the relation of keys'.

This interest in musical theory affected Forster's writing; the transformation and return of phrases was an art he practised with success in his novels, and the relations of keys was also a matter of special interest. He disclaimed expert familiarity with the key-system, but he had a particular fondness, or respect, for C minor, as he explained in an essay called 'The C minor of that life'. He borrowed the title from Browning's poem 'Abt Vogler', the last line of which begins with the words 'The C major of this life'; but C major, perhaps too commonplace, too Victorian, or just insufficiently élite, was not a Forsterian key.

In Browning's poem the organist is extemporizing, building a temple or palace of keys and reflecting that such structures are made out of nothing yet constitute a uniquely beautiful and satisfying order. This is very much what Forster conceives to be the task of all art. He ponders the association of particular keys with particular moods and colours. 'Is there any *absolute* difference between keys – a difference that is inherent, not relative?' he asked Britten, who replied that until equal temperament arrived early in the eighteenth century all the difference rested in higher or lower; however, the slight changes of value brought about in the achieving of equal temperament, which had necessitated small alterations in the intervals between notes, so that the common chords of different keys were now spaced slightly differently, 'gives them slightly different characters'. And as long as these differences exist we may not only attribute different moods, et cetera, to different keys, but attach to a particular key a significance that arises from its association with a particular composer. For instance, Forster enjoyed pointing out that in Wagner's *Ring* the gods go up to Valhalla in C sharp minor, and – hours later – fall back from it in the same key. He wrote in *Two Cheers for Democracy* that *Tristan and Isolde* ended in the key of E major, but then he discovered that it really ended in B major, not a favourite key of his, or Beethoven's; so he crossed out the passage in proof.

C minor is the key of several of Beethoven's most famous works, including the Fifth Symphony, the Third Piano Concerto, and – with a special significance for Forster – the Opus 111 piano sonata. He was obviously keen to find more instances of C minor in Beethoven, and he noted several; indeed Britten teased him for finding a C minor movement in the third Razumovsky quartet where there isn't one. His interest in the key is such that one wonders why he didn't test his opinion of this majestic tonality in composers other than Beethoven, for there are impressive and accessible instances elsewhere; but as far as I can see he left no record of interest in C minor works by other composers. It was odd to pass by Mozart's Piano Concerto No. 24 (K 491), which not only is fine but was certainly well known to Beethoven; and the beautiful slow movement of the E flat major Sinfonia Concertante for violin and viola, which is also in C minor, the related minor. But, strangely, he seems to have thought of Mozart as a mere tinkler. So C minor he shared with Beethoven alone.

In October 1901 he wrote to his friend the musicologist Edward Dent, from the Albergo Bonciani in Florence, reporting that 'the Bonciani pen [presumably the one he was using at the time] is rather bad. Their piano though is rather good'. The Bonciani is generally taken to be the model for the Pensione Simi in *A Room with a View* (though P.N. Furbank records a room-changing incident in another *pensione* involving Forster, Dent and Percy Lubbock). More interesting at present is the fact that the good Bonciano piano turns up in *A Room with a View* and Lucy Honeychurch chooses to play on it the last of Beethoven's piano sonatas, Opus 111 in C Minor. She plays only the first of the two movements, with vigour but inaccurately, though she has played it before, in the hearing of Mr Beebe in Tunbridge Wells.

One way or another Forster achieved a considerable knowledge of the classical repertoire. He was probably better informed than many of his contemporaries. Perhaps he was also more sensitive. In his youth means of listening to music were of course much rarer than they became in the second half of his life. But he played arrangements of orchestral music for piano for four hands, an important source of musical knowledge. As a young man he travelled to Dresden for the first of his many *Rings* and he often went to concerts and operas in London. His enthusiasm for Wagner eventually cooled, but at seventy-five he was once more in Bayreuth and provided a genial but critical account of the visit in 'Revolution at Bayreuth', an essay reprinted in the collection *The Prince's Tale*.

It was not until his later years that recorded music became anything like as available, or carried as much musical information, as now. He hadn't the resources of Proust, who was rich and could summon famous musicians to play to him at midnight in his cork-lined room. And Proust also had his 'théâtrophone', on which he could listen over a telephone line to live performances from the Opéra without even getting up.

Britten notes that Forster's early musical education took place in the nineteenth century, so his taste reflected that fact. Perhaps when he gave Forster a gramophone he was hoping to modernize his taste. Doubtless it was a good machine, but Forster must already have owned one, since he used one during the war when he was working on the Beethoven sonatas. In any case he showed some interest in twentieth-century music, noting, for example, that Ralph Vaughan Williams's Fourth Symphony made him weep. His views were not absolutely conventional; he dared to dislike *Tristan and Isolde* and, though he was not without interest in singing, seems to have ignored Schubert. He agreed with George Bernard Shaw that Haydn might have been capable of tragedy but backed away from it. Forster seems not to have elaborated this judgement – he makes no musicological allusions to the *Sturm und Drang* period – but brief as it is, his judgement reflects a recurrent interest in ideas about the association of greatness and death. Of this I shall have more to say in the next chapter.

Recorded music cannot have contributed to Forster's novels, all of which were written by 1924; electrical recording did not come in until 1925. Even in the 1930s there were only three-to-five minutes of music on each side of a record, which would make any recorded opera, to say nothing of *Götter-dämmerung*, an unwieldy heap of plastic. The twelve-inch so-called long-playing record, which gave twenty minutes a side, arrived in the late 1940s, and stereo recordings were first commercially released only in 1958. Of course Forster knew nothing of the CD or the DVD. But he went to Promenade concerts, sharing a season ticket with friends. We know he heard Sir Henry Wood conducting Beethoven's Fifth Symphony on 26 April 1908, not so long before it starred in *Howards End*. Altogether he did hear quite a lot of music, especially opera: Gluck, Debussy, Charpentier. He liked chamber music and continued to think well of César Franck.

He once wrote a piece suggesting that it was not good to know too much about music – but this reflects an opinion he held or professed to hold about the arts in general, including literature. He believed that the practice of scholarship thwarted the passion with which reading ought to be done. 'Study teaches us everything about a book,' he argued, 'except the central thing.' For related reasons he deplored the practice of fitting 'programmes' to music, a habit that is discussed in that celebrated chapter of *Howards End*. Beethoven's Coriolan Overture was a favourite of his until he discovered that Wagner had fitted it out with a programme: the opening bars suggesting the hero's decision to destroy the Volscii, and the 'sweet tune' that follows indicating 'female influence', succeeded by 'the dotted-quaver restlessness of indecision', presumably indecision about whether to seek the votes of the plebeians or to attack Rome.

In accepting Wagner's programme, said Forster, he had lost his own Coriolan: 'its largeness and freedom have gone'. So he wrote in 1939, but when King's College, thirty years later, put on an orchestral concert to celebrate his ninetieth birthday he chose to open the proceedings with the Coriolan Overture. Perhaps the play itself, with its thwarted hero and oppressive mother, meant something special to him personally. The other items on the celebratory programme were César Franck's

Symphonic Variations and four assorted Lieder (by Brahms, Hugo Wolf, whose 'Ganymed' he particularly admired, and Richard Strauss: no Schubert). The concert ended with Haydn's Trumpet Concerto. Patrick Wilkinson says that Forster's choice was restricted by the performers available, but if there were present orchestral forces equal to playing the Beethoven and the Franck there was surely a broader repertoire to choose from. In his Commonplace Book Forster put a cryptic but almost reverent note of admiration for Brahms's Variations on a Theme of Haydn, in which he detected a rare, precious combination of passion and scholarship; but they were not chosen on this great occasion.

As we've seen, he had his favourites. For Mozart, as I've said, he cared little. Schumann has a bit part in *A Room with a View*. The music of Gustav Mahler, in a damning judgement, Forster described as 'serious but not profound', except for Das Lied von der Erde, which owed its acquittal to performances by the contralto Kathleen Ferrier, whom he may well have known, as she was close to Britten in the post-war years ('and though I tried to dismiss as irrelevant her early death I could not do so').

However, the composers who made a significant contribution to Forster's novels were Beethoven and Wagner. Wagner crops up in *The Longest Journey* and 'The Celestial Omnibus'. Here and there, a third figure, this time an imaginary friend but with his own importance, joins the other two: the great French composer Vinteuil, but he was of course an invention of Proust's. I will say a word or two about these three musicians.

First, Beethoven. As I've suggested, opinions differ about the passage in *Howards End* that Britten commended so warmly, and to me so mysteriously. After answering the question whether one likes the programme or programmes Forster ascribed to the Fifth Symphony, one should attempt the more radical question: has the programme any business at all to be there? Forster avoids serious comment on these important issues by a familiar retreat into drollery. Easy fun is made at the expense of Tibby, fussing about 'the transitional passage on the drum'; further joking about other false or strained attitudes to the music is fine. But the talk of Beethoven's conjuring up shipwrecks and elephants and goblins is an enemy of the music: 'A triumphant conclusion, but the goblins were there. They could return. He had said so bravely, and that is why one can trust Beethoven when he says other things.' I admit to my inability to write down those words without wincing a little. They make me wonder if I can trust Forster when he writes other things. Then it strikes me that he is just being droll.

There is an instance of amiable drollery in the conversation at the Schlegels' luncheon party in the ninth chapter of *Howards End*. The course of the river Oder is said to be like a symphonic poem, the part by the landing stage in B minor, the exit into the Baltic in C sharp. One remembers how much store Forster set by humour in the English novel, though he felt it somehow went awry in Meredith and that in its enfeebled form it had to be killed off by D.H. Lawrence, a difficult writer whom Forster nevertheless seriously and perceptively admired.

Many fanciful programmes have been devised for Beethoven, and the practice may be tolerable – after all he made one himself for the Sixth Symphony – but this one about the Fifth Symphony rings false, and it also provides unhappy examples of the recurrent sermonizing that rather disfigures this novel. The tone is wrong, vaguely facetious, *faux-naïf*; it has what seems intended to be a serious point, but the point is made with a touch of what Forster's friend William Plomer admiringly called his 'lambent playfulness' – a habit that was characterized rather more severely by a friendly critic of Forster's, John Beer, who remarked that language of this sort may war against the 'serious point'.

In an essay called 'Word-making and Sound-taking' (1935), Forster discusses some remarks of the novelist-potter William de Morgan on 'a tune by Beethoven', apparently a passage from the Waldstein Sonata, a work that, as we've seen, he knew well. He claims that this tune suggests to the listener the words 'No, no, you're quite mistaken,/ No, no, you must be wrong'. The tune is of the kind that you can't get out of your head – what I'm told the Germans call 'ear-worms'. Forster goes on to provide some examples of his own setting of words to classical tunes. He takes the terrific subject in Brahms's Variations and Fugue on a Theme by Handel and sings these words to it: 'There was a bee/ Upon a wall,/ and it said buzz and that was all;/ And it said buzz and that was all.' As Forster cheerfully remarks, Proust, who made so much of his own little ear-worms, would have winced at this. My irritation is worsened by my inability to make the words fit the tune, surely the least one might expect.

However, it's meant as a joke, like others of the kind ('O Ebenezer Prout, you're a funny little man', and so on). Forster says 'these capricious insertions of words, parallels, images, jokes, ideas, make listening to music a rocky and romantic affair, and I am very glad that there are also times when I seem to be alone with the sounds.' 'Music,' he says in another place, 'music which is untrammelled and untainted by reference is obviously the best sort of music to listen to; we get nearer the centre of reality.' Here his view is close to the one he gives Margaret Schlegel in *Howards End*, but Helen's raptures about the Fifth Symphony seem almost to become disconnected from her; the 'Panic and emptiness! Panic and emptiness!' she senses, and her endorsement of Beethoven's method of dealing with them, seem, until she rushes out of the concert hall with Leonard Bast's umbrella, to belong not to Helen but to the author.

Forster may not subscribe to the goblin interpretations, but he does believe that great music has 'a message'. 'There's an insistence in music – expressed largely through rhythm; there's a sense that it is trying to push across to us something which is neither an aesthetic pattern nor a sermon. That's what I listen for specially.' And this avowal, as I hope we shall see, is a matter of considerable importance to anybody who wants to know about Forster's practice as a novelist as well as a music lover.

Perhaps chief among the items regarded as having, in this sense, a message, is Beethoven's Piano Sonata Opus 111 in C Minor, to which I shall now for a moment return. This is the music played by Lucy Honeychurch in *A Room with a View*. Britten said he was surprised at the choice of this work, surprised that such a 'muddled little person' as Lucy should choose it and be able to play it. But he claimed to understand that Forster knew what he was doing. The author does not ask us to believe that Lucy played the sonata correctly: 'She was no dazzling *exécutante*, her runs were not at all like strings of pearls, and she struck no more right notes than was suitable for one of her age and situation.' (This is Forster's usual whimsical cover-up but perhaps it makes the choice even more surprising. Lucy doesn't tackle the long 'winding intricacy' of the strange second movement, but the first, with what Forster calls 'its opening dive into the abyss', which is far from being the kind of thing you'd expect an average suburban player to sit down and casually perform. Did she know the movement by heart? Or had she brought a score to

Florence? Or did the *pensione* keep one handy, expecting musical guests?)

Mr Beebe remembers having heard Lucy play it at some charity occasion in Tunbridge Wells, when he had been expecting nothing more exciting than an arrangement of 'Adelaide' or 'The Ruins of Athens'. Now, hearing her do it again on the piano of the *pensione*, he utters a prophecy: 'If Miss Honeychurch ever takes to live as she plays, it will be very exciting – both for us and for her.' If we think of the structure of the whole book we see that this remark of Beebe's is the real reason for introducing Opus III on a wet afternoon in Florence. Lucy's performance presages what we shall quite soon learn to recognize as a 'happening'. The character of the music suggests a message. It is primarily about Lucy Honeychurch, a commonplace girl who can be wonderfully set apart by this music from the ordinary world, the world of her mother. Forster is fond of the agencies by which characters can be set apart in this way, having been set apart himself.

Lucy explains to Mr Emerson that she forgets her worries when playing, which she modestly claims to regard merely as a hobby possibly superior to stamp-collecting. But there is, from the outset, a special insistence on the effect of piano playing on this ordinary girl; 'disjoined from her music-stool [she] was only a young lady with a quantity of dark hair and a very pretty, pale, undeveloped face'. As yet she doesn't live as she plays, but Mr Beebe is prescient.

Much later in his life Forster, speculating whimsically about the future of some of his characters, suggested that during the Second World War Lucy 'gave some music lessons and broadcast some Beethoven'. Anyway, she plays Opus III. Like Britten, we may conquer the feeling that it was a strange choice. In the novel Mr Eager finds it perverse and disturbing, but he is right only, as it were, by accident. His is a voice out of the darkness of middle-class England, and he senses danger or scandal but also fears that something will *happen*. Lucy herself wants 'something big', like Opus 111, and she is about to get it.

On this afternoon in Florence she is 'peculiarly restive'. As a tiny act of defiance she buys some artistic postcards and enters the Piazza Signoria vaguely discontented: 'The world is certainly full of beautiful things, if only I could come *across* them.' (An odd thing to say in Florence, but we have seen she's not very good on art.) 'Nothing ever happens to me,' she thinks. 'An older person ... in such a place,' the narrator remarks, 'might think that sufficient was happening to him, and rest content. Lucy desired more.' 'Then something did happen': she witnesses a murder at close hand. The victim leans towards Lucy and vomits blood. As he is taken away her friend George Emerson appears, 'looking at her across the spot where the man had been. How very odd! Across something.' She has come *across* something. She faints, thinking 'Oh, what have I done?' and then comes to, repeating, 'Oh, what have I done?' Emerson is still looking at her, but this time we are told, 'not *across* anything'*. Emerson says 'imperiously: "The man is dead – the man is probably dead; sit down till you are rested."' When she sends him to retrieve her postcards, covered in blood, he throws them into the river. He says, 'something tremendous has happened; I must face it without getting muddled. It isn't exactly that a man has died ... It has happened, and I mean to find out what it is.' The narrator repeats George's words like a chorus; 'It was not exactly that a man had died; something had happened to the living.'

* Both 'Across something' and 'not across anything' were added by Forster to the typescript. As Stallybrass notes, he was inserting 'thematic links' (*The Lucy Novels*, p. 131).

Lucy thinks, 'Oh, what have I done?' and repeats the question aloud, her own tragic chorus. Though she has done nothing obvious, only fainted, she seems convinced she has 'done' something decisive. 'Again the thought occurred to her, "Oh, what have I done?" – the thought that she, as well as the dying man, had crossed some spiritual boundary.' But she retreats, imagining she can return to the old ways as she knew them before she did whatever it was she had done, before 'something happened' – before the murder, the blood, and the embrace of her rescuer. 'How quickly these accidents do happen,' she says, 'and then one returns to the old life!' This is an attempt to dispose of the happening as merely an accident; but Emerson insists that 'something tremendous has happened': and he wants to face it without getting muddled. 'It isn't exactly that a man has died. ... It has happened ... and I mean to find out what it is.' Again the choric narrator repeats his words. And at the end of the chapter Lucy – who earlier in the afternoon had elicited from the 'little draped piano, the good piano ... the roar of the opening theme of Opus 111' – now, after all the significant happenings, Lucy leant on the parapet and 'contemplated the River Arno, whose roar was suggesting some unexpected melody to her ears'. The word 'roar', used earlier of Beethoven's music, is used now about the rain-swollen river. The something that happened is obscurely related to the piano sonata.

You could read these pages, with all their instances of 'cross' and 'across', of 'happen' and 'happening', 'do' and 'done', all these very ordinary words, without suspecting that the narrative is being made to carry a secret sense, tacitly informing you of the existence and importance of that spiritual boundary, how it is approached, how crossed or shunned; and whether, having crossed it, one can go back.

Her mother thinks music makes Lucy 'peevish' and 'touchy'.

On an insider's view she might rather be thought of as sensitive; as one who can avoid a future in the dark by crossing a boundary from which there should be no return; as an artist, a member of a Forsterian élite. The murder seems to shock her only for a moment, but despite her resistance she is obscurely aware of crossing a spiritual boundary, like the dead man. That, somehow, is what has *happened*, that is what has been so irretrievably *done*. When she thinks of her home it is as a place where 'nothing ever *happened* to her'. When thinking of the murder 'she did not know what had *happened*,' only that something of great importance has occurred, has been done.

The abnormal frequency of the word 'happen' is offset by the forced oddness, in this passage, of the word 'across'. There was nothing subconscious about the repetitions and the seeming inaptness of this word (though Forster trusted the gifts of sleep and unconscious thought and image), for here we find him quite deliberately labouring at the words in his revisions. The words – 'across', 'happen', and, less conspicuously, 'done' – are a form of music, commonplace in themselves as unordered sound, but a tune, a phrase, an earworm; the effect is in some ways comparable to the Vinteuil moments in Proust, and suggesting reasons why those moments later became so fascinating to Forster, perhaps also why he was interested in ear-worms. Somewhere behind their play is Opus 111, a work marking that spiritual boundary. Forster might have approved of Alfred Brendel's description of the sonata as 'a last word leading into silence forever', a sombre confrontation with death, a spiritual boundary.

Having seen how these words worked together Forster inserted more of them. It is of some interest to look at the manuscripts of his earlier attempts at this novel (it was the first he began, though the third to be published). In an early version of the murder in the Piazza Lucy doesn't appear at all. It is Arthur (the original of George Emerson) who walks into the Piazza. Already preceding him is the word 'across'. 'He <began to cross/was crossing> to the entrance of the Uffizi arcade in the opposite corner when there was a sudden concourse on all sides to the great Fountain of Neptune. At the same moment he saw a great red patch by the Loggia ... A line of red spots so large and so near together that those who were returning to the Lung'Arno hotels had either to stride boldly over them [the blood-spots] or find their way back by circuitous lanes.' Arthur hurries to the fountain, on the rim of which lies, almost naked, a handsome young Italian man dripping blood. He passes, in the arcade, 'an American girl' who has trodden in the blood.

Arthur's reaction to this experience is a decision to give up art ('it is so utterly inadequate' to the experience of blood and death). Next day Lucy at last goes to the Piazza and visits the scene of the crime, where she finds Miss Lavish planning a romantic novel based on the quarrel and the murder. She now catches Arthur's mood and finds herself thinking about art and death.

In this early version the happening of the death of the handsome young man in the Piazza means a lot to Arthur but not much to Lucy, and something of that emphasis lingers in the final version. But now Lucy is of course the centre of attention; it is to her at least as much as to George that 'something has happened'.

The judicious narrator remarks that 'they had come to a situation where character tells, and where Childhood enters upon the branching paths of Youth'. This is the sort of intrusive sermonizing, what seems a defiant and ruinous failure of tone, that modern readers of Forster have been taught to object to, and the worst of it is that it has no real connection with the preceding scene. What we can learn from that scene is not a moral concerning 'character' and the branching paths of Youth, but what Forster meant, in his lectures, by 'rhythm'. The repetition of 'happen' is, given the ordinariness of the word, likely to escape notice; with 'across' inattention is hardly possible, for its oddity is forced on us, it cannot escape notice. Both are 'rhythms'.

The *Paris Review* interviewers asked Forster whether he was always aware of his own 'technical cleverness'. He was, of course, but he believed that some clever-looking effects might come about by creative accident; and as he preferred creative accident to conscious forethought he answered them thus: 'People will not realise how little conscious one is of these things, how one flounders about ...' One may pause to admire some careful structural arrangements in his novels: why is Gino's maid Perfetta, in *Where Angels Fear to Tread*, described as unable to find her way about the small town of Monteriano? Not because, or not just because, it was good to have a dull-witted Italian maid in the book for 'colour', but in order that, during the final crisis, she will arrive too late, bearing milk for the baby, already dead. Readers will know other instances of careful plotting: think, in *A Passage to India*, of the anecdote of Aziz's collar-stud, or his game of polo with the subaltern, or Godbole's disastrous puja as the train leaves for Marabar. Virginia Woolf spoke of Forster's 'combination of realism and mysticism' – the realism, roughly, depending on conscious work, the mysticism on creative accident, though of course the two are not always easily distinguished.

Forster believed in inspiration as virtually a daily occurrence; pick up the pen and the flow begins. In the Introduction to the 1947 edition of his *Collected Stories* he muses on this topic. It happens: sometimes it works, and sometimes it doesn't. An inspired passage may be followed by one for which no claim to inspiration may be made, but it is unlikely that anybody will detect the seam where the inspired and the uninspired meet. 'All a writer's faculties, including the valuable faculty of faking, do conspire together thus for the creative act, and often do contrive an even surface, one putting in a word here, another there.' Among those words lurk the rhythms.

What is here meant by 'faking'? *OED* allows that the word has musical meanings – for instance, the arrangement of a piece for instruments – say saxophone and banjo – other than those specified in the score. Sometimes, used of jazz, it means little more than 'improvisation'. Alexander Goehr tells me it can also refer to the stratagems of performers when confronted with something almost or quite impossible to play as written, for example some late writing for horns by Richard Strauss. I feel sure I've heard the word applied to some benign trickery employed in the process of composition, but Goehr doesn't endorse this usage. All the same, it could be a way of describing the tricks by which a novelist might bypass an awkward moment in the narrative – or plant the notes of those occult tunes, the senses under the sense that music achieves by recall, by transformations, by exploiting the relations of keys, and so on.

The manuscripts of *A Room with a View* suggest that the Piazza scene was a particularly important and difficult moment, somewhat resembling the crisis Forster experienced in writing *A Passage to India*, when he knew that the Caves had to be got through, that something important had to happen there before he could get on; yet despite many attempts he could not find the solution for years, and in the end provided it by what could be called inspired creative faking. In much the same way the Piazza stood in the way and had to be dealt with by creative inspired faking. What Forster had to do was to attach the action to a decisive experience of the right characters; originally the scene contained neither of them and then only the young man. Both had boundaries to cross, both wanted something to happen. The casual killing and the bloody postcards made it possible to develop these themes. Lucy will try to return to the old ways, but finally cannot, and she emerges from the ordeal as the kind of human being who is acceptable to the novelist.

That Opus 111 played a part – *happened* to play a part – in getting her across that boundary is the result of faking. Forster remodelled the Piazza scene to enshrine what he had now discovered to be the theme of the book, and to accommodate pre-echoes of the finale. Why the American girl and her blood-stained shoes were involved I haven't discovered.

For long a fervent Wagnerian – his first name for Stephen Wonham in *The Longest Journey* was Siegfried – Forster came in time to regard the leitmotivs of *The Ring* as a bit blatant, incessantly directing one's attention to ring, sword, Valhalla, and so on. He admitted to his interviewers that he had learned from the Wagnerian leitmotivs, but his own 'rhythms', as he called them in *Aspects of the Novel*, are less obtrusive. You are not meant always to know whether they are intended or not. The games he plays with 'happen' and with 'across'– much subtler, I think, than the rhythms of *Howards End* and even those of *The Longest Journey*, though less impressive than those of *A Passage to India* – indeed must owe something to Wagner. They cannot be indebted to Proust because Proust wasn't available in 1908. But eventually Proust, and the fictional composer Vinteuil, became very important to the business of faking rhythms.

Forster bought a copy of *Du Côté de Chez Swann* – the first part of Proust's novel, published in 1913 – at Marseille, on his way home from his second Indian visit. A diary entry speaks of its almost immediate effect on his Indian novel, then in progress. (It is of some interest that another book that stimulated him during the final writing of *A Passage to India* was T.E. Lawrence's *Seven Pillars of Wisdom*; he had a certain longing for the heroic, for Coriolanus, for the extraordinarily active life, the more so when it coexisted with the contemplative or was contrasted, for example, with the unheroic yet productive Proust in his cork-lined room.) And Proust thought of music as Forster did: as the deepest, most transcendent of the arts, as well as a most powerful agent of memory.

In the discussion of rhythms in *Aspects of the Novel* Forster explains the role in the novel of the composer Vinteuil's *petite phrase:* It 'has a life of its own ... it is almost an actor, but not quite ... Its power has gone towards stitching Proust's book from the inside ... There are times when the little phrase – from its gloomy inception, through the sonata into the septet, means everything to the reader. There are times when it means nothing and is forgotten; and this seems to me the function of rhythm in fiction: not to be there all the time like a pattern [as in James] but by its lovely waxing and waning to fill us with surprise and freshness and hope.' This is a good account of the way Forster worked.

There is much argument about the origin of Vinteuil's little phrase. It may derive from a rather inferior sonata by Saint-Saëns or from something by Fauré; or it may be borrowed from the Good Friday music in *Parsifal*; or the shepherd's piping at the beginning of the last act of *Tristan*; or – to me the happiest, if not the most probable conjecture – it may come from Beethoven's Opus 111 – though from the second movement, neglected or shirked by Lucy.

Anyway, the phrase has been composed by Proust's composer, who has died in obscurity. At the outset of the great novel the violin sonata is a matter of secondary interest; attention is paid rather to the immoral life of Vinteuil's daughter. When Swann becomes fascinated with a *petite phrase* in the sonata it does not seem to him that its composer can possibly be the country organist he knew of as Vinteuil. He comes to associate it with his love for Odette. It becomes 'the national anthem' of their affair and prompts a fascinating discourse on memory. Vinteuil is discovered and made fashionable; meanwhile the sonata has developed splendidly, first into a quartet, then a sextet, then a septet, a grander work by far – an acknowledged masterpiece. It is strongly associated with *Tristan*, and Albertine plays parts of it for Swann on the pianola. It reaches its maximum exposure in the final stages of the novel. As I say, it has been found reminiscent of Wagner, Beethoven, Fauré, Franck, Debussy, Saint-Saëns, a whole anthology of ear-worms.

When Forster was writing *Aspects of the Novel* he did not know Proust's final volume, *Le Temps retrouvé*, which was published posthumously in 1927; he felt sure the best of the novel was over and did not agree with people who thought the whole thing would only come together in the end; he claimed that the book was a whole, that it 'hangs together because it is stitched internally. Because it contains rhythms.' This is an important idea, for it means that a novel need not comply with conventional temporal restrictions; it hardly even needs to end, because structural satisfactions are otherwise provided for. Neither Forster nor Proust could actually quite dispense with conventional temporal sequence, or with 'reality effects', but each desired his work to be a whole, and believed that those concealed stitches achieved that wholeness.

That a musical rhythm should be made the source of literary

rhythms impressed Forster, and he would, I think, have liked Julia Kristeva's description of *la petite phrase* as 'enigmatic polyphony'. Knowing only part of Proust's novel, he nevertheless understood the means by which the enormous book 'hangs together'. He had done something like it himself.

No lambent playfulness here. He is talking about something that was of real importance to him. He knew about rhythm, perhaps would have found another and better name for it if it had not been best exemplified by this music of Vinteuil. On the question of whether 'rhythms' must be of spontaneous invention he seems to have been of two minds. In practice the phrases or rhythms may occur spontaneously, but their disposition is the work of conscious choice. Wagner's signature phrases are intentional, conscious; Forster came to think them too obvious, relying rather on inspiration to provide the rhythms. Proust may have developed Wagner's method in much the same way, allowing the little phrase to declare and develop itself much as Vinteuil's sonata becomes a septet. As Forster remarks, Proust can ignore the phrase for hundreds of pages and it will not be missed; or it can seem insistently present, always changing with its context: an enigmatic polyphony indeed.

Committed to a certain realism in his fiction, Forster sought ways to make his novels musical as well as respectful of the manners appropriate to the traditional novel and reasonably acceptable to the unadventurous customer (whom he referred to as Uncle Willie). To achieve that concordance was in part the work of the subconscious – of what he frankly called inspiration.

The rhythms had to be more or less smuggled in. Their presence in Forster's fiction is well known, and much has been written about them, yet they are probably more numerous than most readers realize. Let me end with an example of rhythmical composition, in a single scene from *A Passage to India*.

After the breakdown of the Aziz trial Fielding has rescued Miss Quested and given her refuge in his College. They are joined there by Hamidullah, an intelligent anti-British lawyer, whose anger on behalf of Aziz adds to the awkwardness of the moment. Where is Miss Quested to go? Not to Heaslop and, equally obvious, not to the Turtons. But Fielding is going away – might she stay at the College when Fielding has left? She is ashamed about her false charge against Aziz and her withdrawal of it when the trial was already under way, and asks Fielding, 'Have you any explanation of my extraordinary behaviour?' He has none. Later she says, 'The fact is that I realized before it was too late that I had made a mistake, and had just enough presence of mind to say so. That is all my extraordinary conduct amounts to.' (Forster added the first 'extraordinary' in a late draft.) We remember that from the first sentence of the novel the word is always related to Marabar or to conduct caused by Marabar.

Our ears have by now become accustomed to the repetition of the triadic appeal to Krishna to come. Sometimes this rhythm affects other words, is echoed in remote contexts: 'Madam, madam, madam' or 'kindness, kindness, kindness', but it is firmly associated with the word 'come'. Sometimes it is ironic. Any person, any thing, even a godforsaken landscape, can repeat the plea to Krishna to come, though he declines or neglects to do so. Earlier, at Fielding's tea party, it is Heaslop who comes instead of Krishna: he comes, he comes, he comes – the ugly imperial substitute for the god. Now, as Heaslop once again arrives at the College, Hamidullah marks his advent by saying, 'Here comes the City Magistrate. He comes in a third-class band-ghari for the purposes of disguise, he comes unattended, but here comes the City Magistrate ... He comes, he comes, he comes ...' Hamidullah, a Muslim, has no direct interest in Krishna, and we cannot know (and need not ask) whether he has ever heard the triadic formula used. If you like, you can say it has passed to him as it were telepathically (though we are expressly warned not to depend on that meagre resource), or – better – think of it as an element of the closed system of the book, of its internal stitching.

However, on this occasion Heaslop declines to come; he stops outside on the verandah and Fielding has to go out to him, returning to report to the others that Heaslop 'prefers not to come in'. Adela asks, rather awkwardly, 'Does he tell me to come out to him?' She goes, but Fielding declines to escort her. Hamidullah comments: 'It was insulting of him not to come in', but Fielding is generous, saying 'Heaslop doesn't come out badly' – a rather forced colloquialism, or an abbreviation of the more natural 'doesn't come out of it badly', here honoured because it contains the word 'come'. Now Adela returns and asks Fielding to see Heaslop again: 'Do come and see Ronny again.' But Fielding resists: 'I think he should come in this time', he says, 'feeling that this much was due to his own dignity. "Do ask him to come."' So Heaslop enters, saying, 'I came to bring Miss Quested away', before explaining that he can't.

Now except to provide occasion for all this coming and coming, there was no need to make Heaslop stay on the verandah alone. He arrives at Fielding's college with no power to do anything but accept Fielding's offer to accommodate Adela; he is humiliated and bereaved and in no position to stand on ceremony. But narrative business is modified to accommodate this bit of internal stitching, this half-hidden repetition of the basic rhythm of Krishna's absence and presence.

Later Fielding recalls the moment on the evening before the trial when from the Club verandah 'he saw the fists and fingers of Marabar swell until they included the whole night sky', bringing total darkness. So Marabar, closing in on the imperial outpost, also comes. Mrs Moore, called by the mob by her divine name, neglects to come. The stitching is beautiful, the work of an imagination that might well be called musical, passionate and complicated, as Forster thought art should be.

3 Krishna

'Death destroys a man; the idea of Death saves him.' Behind the coffins and the skeletons that stay the vulgar mind lies something so immense that all that is great in us responds to it. Men of the world may recoil from the charnel-house that they will one day enter, but Love knows better. Death is his foe, but not his peer, and in their age-long struggle the thews of Love have been strengthened, and his vision cleared, until there is no one who can stand against him.

Howards End

Lionel Trilling's remark that Forster refused greatness is often quoted, and was no doubt worth making, especially if taken along with many tributes suggesting that greatness refused to be refused. In fact greatness seems to have been a topic of exceptional interest to this modest man. It shows up often, in and out of the novels. Forster occasionally gave some thought to his own size, deciding, for instance, that he was larger than Virginia Woolf – though that was in 1915, when four of his novels had been published while she, though promising, was just beginning. Later he was willing to regard Woolf as a great novelist but uncertain whether she could also be called a great critic, a question he settled only when inserting 'great' before 'critic' on his proof.

In another place he wondered whether Edward Carpenter, some aspects of whose life and doctrines he at one time profoundly approved, and who was indirectly the inspiration for his novel *Maurice*, could truly be called great. And he was exercised by the question of André Gide's possible greatness: he knew Gide and had a slightly chilly respect for him as a man and understood 'how much he had got out of life ... Not life's greatness – greatness is a nineteenth-century perquisite, a Goethean job. [Gide] had not a great mind. But he had a free mind, and free minds are as rare as great.' Nevertheless he remembered that Gide had left him sitting in a restaurant while he departed without attending to the bill.

As I've already remarked, Forster approved of Shaw's judgement on Haydn: that he missed greatness by shunning the tragic; otherwise he 'would have been among the greatest'. I repeat this plausible and attractive observation because it raises the question of the connection, in Forster, of the ideas of greatness and tragedy or death.

Coming to terms with death, he believed, was a necessary element in the idea of greatness. In a letter to G.L. Dickinson written during the period when he was working on *A Passage to India* and not making much progress, Forster complained crossly about 'the studied ignorance of novelists' and added that 'they must recapture their interest in death'. Death may seem to be the antithesis of that 'creative state' which he so valued and which he believed necessary to the production of art; but when – to use a favourite figure of Forster's – when its buckets are raised up from the subconscious, when its *trouvailles* are mixed with worldly information, creativity will not offer a true report if it neglects death. Art is based, he said (and it may be his most important dictum), 'on an integrity in man's nature which is deeper than moral integrity'. At that lower level of integrity death is essential, and to exclude it from the creative effort is to thwart creativity and deny greatness.

*

Perhaps Forster had no occasion and no need to express these notions in any very definite way – or perhaps he had a need not to do so – but their importance is undeniable. One has only to think of the Marabar episode and the tragedy of Mrs Moore in *A Passage to India*. In an early manuscript of the novel her illness besets her in the purdah carriage of the train taking the party to the Marabar hills, and she is too unwell even to enter a cave; but it must have been evident to Forster from the outset that some more serious encounter with fear and sickness was needed at this point, and the panic in the cave was both stronger in itself and more germane to the entire episode.

The most remarkable bit of worrying about death and greatness in Forster's novels is the scene in *The Longest Journey* just after the death of Agnes's fiancé, Gerald, where Rickie urges Agnes to respond passionately to this event. Like other characters in Forster, she has been experiencing 'an obscure spiritual crisis', not knowing whether to grieve demonstratively like the servants or reflect that the death of a man might not be such a great matter after all. (It is a version of the situation in the Piazza scene of *A Room with a View* which I discussed in the last chapter: death causes these crises.) Agnes, like Lucy before her, has 'invited herself to apathy'. But Rickie disapproves and bursts wildly in on her. She asks him to go away. He says he will, but insists on staying: 'Yes, dear Agnes, of course; but I must first see that you mind.' ... 'It's the worst thing that can ever happen to you in all your life, and you've got to mind it – you've got to mind it.' He goes on talking like this for a while. 'Mind it!' he repeats. Agnes is impressed by the urgency of his counsel: 'Through all her misery she knew that this boy was greater than they supposed.' He tells her, 'It's your death as well as his. He's gone, Agnes, and his arms will never hold you again. In God's name mind such a thing ... Don't stop being great; that's the one crime he'll never forgive you.' And a little later, 'He is in heaven, Agnes, the greatest thing is over.' In fact he tells her this twice, and it seems that heaven is relevant, even though nothing really great can be expected of it. And the remark itself shows what Agnes regards as a surprising certainty on the point, coming from Rickie.

This is certainly one of the most intensely written scenes in all of Forster's novels; and it is underlined in a rather curious way when Agnes tempts Rickie into his sacred Madingley dell and kisses him again; he instructs her not to forget that her 'greatest thing is over. What I said to you then is greater than what I say to you now. What he gave you then is greater than anything you will get from me.' Agnes is 'frightened,' and 'again she had the sense of something abnormal'. Well she might, for this is a strange moment, introduced mysteriously – 'no sign, neither angry motion of the air nor hint of January mist', but with signs that by yielding to Agnes Rickie is somehow betraying the dead Gerald and ending 'the tragedy that he had deemed immortal'. Or had he died for Gerald? At first he has not wanted to follow her into the dell ('the devil had done much, but he should not take him to her') but he gives in and then finds himself 'sitting down with his head on her lap. He had laid it there for a moment before he went out to die, and she had not let him take it away.' The scene is virtually a Spenserian allegory, with Agnes as Acrasia and Rickie as Guyon, or rather some Ariostan knight who succumbs to the temptress in just such a dell. A hundred pages later, when Agnes, 'robust and practical', is displaying her efficiency in school business, they never so much as mention Gerald, but he hopes she secretly thinks of him, and of 'the greatest moment of her life'. It is by now an empty expression, Agnes being the nonentity she is to Ansell and not the tragic heroine imagined by Rickie.

Trilling describes as 'fine' the scene in which Rickie introduces his notion of 'minding', and speaks of Agnes's 'one moment of greatness'; and Trilling is a critic whose perceptions are usually fine. But he also admires Ansell's histrionic outburst in the school dining-hall, describing it as 'impossible but rather superb'; he clearly had a taste for those moments in Forster that seem to others falsely operatic and embarrassing. (Benjamin Britten, it must be admitted, found it operatic and not in the least embarrassing.) It is quite hard to make out, behind the passionate repetitions, just what Rickie means; all we can really feel about it is that it is *meant* to be very important; that we, as well as Agnes, are being rather obscurely urged to *mind* about death in order to be *great*. Gerald, Rickie, Agnes are all great, according to some unstated and capacious definition of the term. Greatness, it appears, comes confusedly from the acceptance of death as monstrous, final, unbearable but necessary to be borne with courage – something great in itself that the less-than-great tend to back away from, inviting themselves to apathy, refusing to *mind*. By forcefully pointing this out, and offering unexpected Christian consolation, Rickie himself is seen as achieving an unexpected measure of greatness.

In *Where Angels Fear to Tread*, a novel we may think lighter in tone, Forster offers more odd and suggestive instances of this theme. Thinking that Gino has sold his only son to Harriet, Philip says, 'Poor Gino ... He's no greater than I am, after all.' Philip is an ordinary fellow, only fairly nice and cultivated, with no claim at all to be great, while Gino has seemed to represent a sort of pure peasant greatness before he apparently betrays it by selling his child. Actually he hasn't, so Philip must change his opinion, but he remains preoccupied by vague ideas of greatness: after the accident and the death of the baby he can 'scarcely survey the thing. It was too great.' What made it so was his understanding, more aesthetic than ethical, that in the coach journey 'they were travelling with the whole world's sorrow, as if all the persistency of woe were gathered to a single fount'. The coach is an emblem of universal grief; it proclaims an absolute need to mourn greatly. It belongs to Art, which offers only ambiguous answers: it does not dwell on questions of moral integrity but is meant to appeal rather to that integrity which, Forster remarked, lies deeper. Later Philip perceives in the behaviour of Caroline Abbott evidence 'that there was greatness in the world'. He then resolves 'to be worthy of the things she had revealed'. Touched by greatness, 'he was saved'. 'Life', he later obscurely remarks, 'was greater than he had supposed', though less 'complete'.

Caroline confesses her love for Gino, so Philip loses her. She explains the origin of her love; in a finely wrought scene toward the end of the book she remembers a moment when she prayed they might all return to what they had been before these adventures; but no such return is possible for those who have suffered the pain of being saved, who have greatly experienced the completeness that death brings to life: 'the thing was even greater than she imagined'. Nor had Philip any expectation to be radically changed: he has told Caroline so, admitted his disappointments and his mediocrity: the pleasures of the theatre and of her conversation, he says, were such that he doubts if he will 'ever meet anything greater'. But he is close to the situation of Lucy and George in *A Room with a View*: Caroline says to him, 'I wish something would happen to you, my dear friend; I wish something would happen to you' – repeating the magical statement in the manner of Lucy in the passage I've discussed earlier and, as it were, borrowing the verb from the other book.

Something does happen to Philip, and it has to do with death and loss and the greatness they entail. In the train on the way back to England Caroline says that she herself was saved by Gino's having taken her for a superior being. It seems that both Philip and Caroline are being prepared, in an unexpected way, for a serious future – not a conventionally happy one, that is not the point, and each of them is in obvious ways deprived. That future is for those who have experienced greatness by confronting death and love; for those who at least do not retreat from the spiritual boundary even when not to do so involves an experience of deprivation; for those who are saved.

The tone is evangelical, and commentators quite reasonably relate it to the religious history of Forster's family. There is a connection between the test of greatness and the choice to be made between winning salvation and backsliding. True, some forms of greatness seem not to require a deliberate spiritual or intellectual effort, for it can simply inhere in individuals, like physical beauty or second sight. Mrs Wilcox in *Howards End* 'was not intellectual, not even alert, and it was odd that, all the same, she had greatness'. If Mrs Wilcox has it, so does Mrs Moore in *A Passage to India*. She is a pleasant old woman who happens to become a goddess, meanwhile ceasing to be pleasant. The greatness of neither woman can be explained by anything like conscious effort or desire. It is certainly not a matter of their invariably being nice to people, though that is an admirable trait; it has to do with death – each woman dies in the course of her novel, and their deaths affect the plot and tone of the works. It also has to do with some vaguely secular, rather negative idea of salvation. Things happen to them, there are decisive, life-changing 'happenings', monstrous in Mrs Moore's case, when the universe itself takes the side of death, life-changing for Caroline and Lucy, and for Agnes, if Ricky has his way.

Fielding, in *A Passage to India*, is a strong character, with something of the manner of Leonard Woolf – patient with 'sillies' but himself rational and practical. One imagines him as the sort of man Forster might admire without much liking: decent, intelligent, involved in various actions of moral importance but in none that could be called happenings in this sense. Epiphanies and conversion experiences are obviously a different matter altogether. The parallel of Fielding and Woolf must not be pressed too far; Woolf was Forster's mentor in ways both important and unimportant. He taught Forster to ride before he went off to India, and he offered practical information of particular value to a man who could not believe telephone wires were not hollow. And Forster never forgot that at the time when he was struggling to finish *A Passage to India* it was Woolf who helped him through. Fielding is mature and reasonable, generous and just – if only the English in India had all been like him – but he cannot keep the friendship of Aziz; he is not a *silly* man and not a *saved* man; he would not quite fit into a Forsterian élite, a Carpenterian realm of love, the Beloved Republic that feeds upon freedom and lives. Yet such an élite might well allow entry to the baffling Godbole, or to the enchanting but criminal Maharajah in Forster's memoir, *The Hill of Devi*.

We know from the earlier novels of the existence of spiritual boundaries, lines which can be crossed, to which retreat, if offered, ought to be refused. And we know that if there are to be happenings this is where they must occur. When Hamidullah and Fielding discuss Mrs Moore's death neither can regard it as a happening, which in an obvious way it was for the mob outside the courthouse when they hailed her as a goddess. For the mob, it was an epiphany, certainly bizarre, but an epiphany; and nothing of the sort can be provided to these 'middle-aged men, who had invested their emotions elsewhere'. They have forfeited the chance of greatness. If it can be said in their defence that they were tested by the court case of Aziz it would have to be added that, frustrated by the uproar of the students and the scramble to protect Adela, they backed away. The author gives them an excuse: 'The soul is tired in a moment, and in fear of losing the little she does understand, she retreats to the permanent lines which habit or chance have dictated, and suffers there'. Retreat to the permanent lines is the end of greatness for them, as it would have been for Lucy and Agnes, indeed for anybody.

A hint about the nature of Forster's idea of greatness may be found in his dislike of Henry James, which he expresses a number of times in the course of his writing. In *Aspects of the Novel* he says James's characters 'are gutted of the common stuff that fills characters in other books, and ourselves'. And this castrating is not in the interests of the Kingdom of Heaven; 'there is no philosophy in James's novels, no religion (except an occasional touch of superstition), no prophecy, no benefit for the superhuman at all'. In his Rede Lecture on Virginia Woolf (1941) there is a long gastronomic simile, detecting 'a little too much lamp oil in George Meredith's wine, a little too much paper crackling on Charles Lamb's pork. And no savour whatever in any dish of Henry James.' And we recall once more that he sided with Wells in his quarrel with James – and I cannot think that anything but extraordinary.

Leaving aside the questions whether the artist Forster rightly claimed to be should seek reasons to speak for the enemy against the artist, whether there was nothing to be said, in the case of James, by way of mitigation, it remains true that Forster finds reasons to dislike a form of art that shuns any formula for character that is founded, as his was, on a conception of greatness closely related to the problems of life in an ambiguous universe, and to a particular idea of salvation, or the refusal of salvation. Such a conception of greatness may demand the inclusion of religion, or what Forster calls prophecy, the superhuman. Forster *is* interested in the super-human, and also in what he here calls the Kingdom of Heaven and elsewhere the Beloved Republic, which is also related to his idea of love and the sort of person who is capable of love as he understands it, who also feeds upon freedom and is therefore associated with that ideal realm.

Take, for instance, his un-Jamesian response to the festivities related to the birth of Krishna, which he witnessed in the Indian state where he served. In *The Hill of Devi* he describes a great deal of muddle and foolishness, but he loves his Maha-rajah, an intelligent man who observed extreme courtesy to guests and employees, played childish games, neglected his duties and foolishly ran up debts – a man described by a correspondent of Forster's as 'one of the most loveable, most original and most unwise men I have ever met'. This great man prays frequently to Krishna, keeping in touch, almost minute by minute, with the superhuman. Forster's portrait is affectionate but comic. Compare that record of his time in the chaotic little Indian state with its transformation, or trans-figuration, in the last section of *A Passage to India*: the muddle and the silliness are still there, but whereas in the memoir the emphasis is almost always on Forster's amused tolerance of the goings-on at the festival, the novel, in scenes of ecstatic transformation, calls for Forster's most inspired prose:

> Covered with grease and dust, Professor Godbole had once more developed the life of his spirit. He had, with increasing vividness, again seen Mrs Moore, and round her faintly cling-ing forms of trouble. He was a Brahman, she Christian, but it made no difference, it made no difference whether she was a trick of his memory or a telepathic appeal. It was his duty, as

it was his desire, to place himself in the position of the God and to love her, and to place himself in her position and to say to the God: 'Come, come, come.' This was all he could do. How inadequate! But each according to his own capacities, and he knew his own were small. 'One old Englishwoman and one little, little wasp,' he thought, as he stepped out of the temple into the grey of a pouring wet morning. 'It does not seem much, still, it is more than I am myself.'

The collocation of Mrs Moore and the wasp has long been famous as an exemplary rhythm, and the two could not have been brought together except in the mind of Godbole. When Forster wrote, in a note on *Passage*, that the nine days of his participation in the celebration of Gokal Ashtami and Krishna were 'the strangest and strongest Indian experience granted me', he was presumably remembering the emotion that is again evident in these words of Godbole. It is an emotion that is not registered in the cooler element of *The Hill of Devi*, where Forster's tone is certainly affectionate, but touched by the humour with which he so often veiled what he feared might seem portentous. We may be reasonably sure that the Godbole of the novel incorporates some aspects of Bapu Sahib, who had, as Forster wrote, 'the rare quality of evoking himself', adding, 'I do not believe that he is here doing it for the last time'. We may have here another evocation of greatness.

He insists on the novelist's right to vary the point of view as he chooses or needs. 'I believe a novelist can shift his viewpoint if it comes off ... Indeed, the power to expand and contract perception [is] one of the great advantages of the novel form; and it has a parallel in our perceptions of life.' He also insists, *contra* James, on the novelist's at least occasional access to omniscience. We have seen him exercising his rights by showing intimate knowledge of the workings of Godbole's mind; up to this point Godbole has been pious but evasive on matters of the spirit, but Forster intervenes when he adds those aspects of Bapu Sahib, speaks for Godbole's silent thought, and 'bounces' the reader into acceptance, as he once put it. Here is the funny old fellow whose praying causes Fielding to miss the train to Marabar; who will not sing when asked to but only when he wants to, just as the guests are leaving; who, when he does want to, sings only of the milkmaid unavailingly beseeching Krishna to come – this after a party at which the absent Krishna's inadequate substitute was Ronnie Heaslop; who can have his happiness wrecked by the sight of a slice of beef on a distant plate; who torments Fielding at the climax of the Aziz affair with talk of finding a name for his new school. Odd, inexplicable, a bit of a joke! But now the clairvoyance induced by his religious ecstasy becomes, as it were, the possession of the novelist. Hitherto Godbole has been at best charmingly odd; now, though he may not in his own estimation amount to much, he has the power to imagine the wholeness of the world and the knowledge that a god may be called upon, may descend and save.

The Maharajah as he appears in *The Hill of Devi* is a droll though morally impressive figure, 'so high spirited, so subtle, and so proud that it was often difficult to know what he felt', displaying a peculiar blend of interests, of Indian mysticism and western technology, and being almost certainly one of the saved (though in worldly terms he came to an unhappy end). Forster reports a conversation during which he told this maharajah of a mishap to a visiting engineer and his wife. The Maharajah's reaction to the story made him 'wonder whether [the Maharajah] might possess supernormal faculties'. The couple were motoring, and just as they crossed a bridge 'some animal or other' dashed out of a ravine and charged the car, which swerved and nearly hit the parapet of the bridge. 'His

Highness was keenly interested. "The animal came from the left?" he asked. "Yes." "It was a large animal? Larger than a pig but not as big as a buffalo?" "Yes, but how did you know?" "You couldn't be sure what animal it was?" "No, we couldn't." He leaned back again and said "It is most unfortunate. Years ago I ran over a man there. ... Ever since he has been trying to kill me in the form you describe." The three of us were awe-struck.'

This glimpse of the superstitious or supernatural is put to extraordinary use in *A Passage to India*. Ronny Heaslop and Adela Quested have just decided against marrying. Offered a ride in the Nawab Bahadur's new car, they reluctantly accept. The Nawab orders the driver to take the Gangavati road. He falls asleep, and Ronny alters the instruction, explaining that the Gangavati road is under repair, and making the man take the Marabar road instead. 'One of the thrills so frequent in the animal kingdom passed between' Ronny and Adela when a jolt causes their hands to touch, and 'a spurious unity descended on them'. Then there is a slight 'bump, jump, a swerve' – the car has collided with a tree; 'an accident ... nobody hurt'. Adela believes the cause was 'a large animal [which] rushed up out of the dark on the right and hit us'. In her excitement she obscures whatever animal tracks may have been on the road – a buffalo? a hyena? – sweeping 'her skirts about until it was she, if any one, who appeared to have attacked the car'.

The Nawab remarks that the crash would not have occurred if the driver had taken the Gangavati road as he had ordered. But the Marabar road was sinister, running through a poor landscape where there was 'not enough god to go round'. The lovers touch hands and the engagement is renewed. They tell their news to Mrs Moore and also tell her about the accident on the road and their theories about what caused it. 'Mrs

Moore shivered, "A ghost!"' She does not know, the chauffeur hadn't known, but the Nawab knows that years before at that place he had driven his car 'over a drunken man and killed him, and the man had been waiting for him ever since' – the same response as the Maharajah in Forster's memoir, but the Nawab does not confide this information to an Englishman, as the Maharajah was willing to do.

There are passages in this novel that encourage one to borrow Rickie's expression and speak of its greatness. This incident on the Marabar road is one such. In some respects it is Proustian, but it may be better to say that it is faithful to the details of life and character, as Forster believed novelists ought to be, yet imaginatively irradiated. The Nawab's ghost is not dismissed as mere superstition – in fact its ghostliness is, so to speak, validated by Mrs Moore's reaction to the news. Making Ronny responsible for the change from the Gangavati to the Marabar road has a double justification: we have seen that it is the sort of high-handed thing he would do anyway, and we already know something about the Marabar road. It is, in its unassertive way, *extraordinary*. 'Trees of a poor quality bordered the road, indeed the whole scene was inferior ... In vain did each item in it call out "Come, come."' The road is void of Krishna; any unity it might have proposed would be spurious. And here is something possibly to be thought of as evil – the extraordinary, unidentifiable animal. Miss Quested's sweeping her skirts about muddles and confuses the evidence; she will do the same later when she claims to have been attacked by an unidentified assailant in the cave, the equivalent of the unidentified beast. The Marabar road is a negation leading to a negation; its power to do evil produces the bad sex of this car journey and, in the end, the mystery of the assault on Adela. In an early manuscript Mrs Moore asks her, 'When did you and Ronny come to your understanding?

Was it after the animal attacked your car or before?' Forster deleted this, but what it says is important: Mrs Moore suspects it was the burst of violence on this road that brought them together sexually. Possibly Forster thought the remark too intrusive, out of character for Mrs Moore, or perhaps he felt he had already done enough about the Marabar road; anyway he left this out.

It is well known that Forster wrote *A Passage to India* in two phases, the first in 1913–14, the second in 1922–4. The scene of the ghostly animal on the Marabar road could not have been written before Forster's second visit to India, during which he heard the Maharajah's story. It was written, therefore, more or less contemporaneously with the scene of the assault in the cave. All we can say is that Forster wanted something to happen that was both sexual and obscurely ugly. In 1914 he apparently couldn't manage it. Many years later he said that at the time he had been 'clear about the chief characters and the racial tension, had visualized the scenery and had foreseen that something crucial would happen in the Marabar Caves. But I hadn't seen far enough.' It can be guessed from the extant manuscripts that he had got some way into the caves; there *was* an assault on Adela, or possibly even a degree of consent on her part: 'Aziz & Janet [Adela] drift into one another's arms – then apart' runs a jotting. In another she 'discovers she loves him' ...

But none of that would do, and Forster could not get past the caves. Before he returned to the problem a decade later he has not only revisited India but had written the then unpublishable *Maurice*. Owing a good deal to the admired Edward Carpenter, who enjoyed a life-long homosexual partnership of the kind Forster so much desired for himself, he could now be bolder, and approach a little closer the standard of sexual candour for which he was to praise Carpenter in an obituary notice for him that he wrote in 1929. There seems little doubt that the eerie little episode on the Marabar road, unlike any account of sex in the earlier novels, except perhaps for the embrace of Rickie and Agnes I have discussed, was made possible by a change for which Carpenter, and the writing of *Maurice*, deserve some credit, though Carpenter, who had celebrated what he called *Love's Coming-of-Age*, might not have used so dark a palette.

I return to Marabar and Krishna, and recall the opening sentence of the novel. 'Except for the Marabar Caves – and they are twenty miles off – the city of Chandrapore presents nothing extraordinary.' In the early manuscript we find, in the place of the last three words, 'offers little of interest'. This sounds like guide-book prose, but the substitution of 'extraordinary' for 'of interest' is inspired faking. The last words of the opening chapter are 'the extraordinary caves' (in the manuscript there are more guidebook words following 'caves', now cut). Thereafter the word 'extraordinary' is used only of the caves and of Miss Quested's conduct when she visits them.

The first words of the book are 'Except for the Marabar Caves'. The usual order of principal and subordinate clauses is reversed, so that the exception gets first mention; the exception is necessary to the whole. In between 'except' and 'extraordinary caves' the chapter speaks of the river Ganges whose plain is interrupted by the rocks, the 'fists and fingers' of Marabar thrusting up through the soil. Later, as I've said, we read that at night the hills with their caves seem to advance on the city. They 'come', even if Krishna doesn't. This short opening chapter is a fine instance of faking, of the operation of the creative spirit, as well as of what are called 'rhythms'.

Later the caves themselves must be confronted. Forster had a model for his caves in the ones at Barabar, but he explains that those caves were Buddhist 'and their entrances are not unornamented'. (In fact they are highly ornamented, and it was a bold stroke on behalf of negativity to strip them bare and deprive them of religion, to make them extra-ordinary.) Mrs Moore has her fright. There is an echo in the caves, a negation in itself or the agent of negation, reducing every word, whether commonplace, poetic or spiritual, to a meaningless boom. The accident to the Nawab's car on the Marabar road is mysterious and, in its effect, evil; on that road there isn't enough god to go round; here, in the caves, there is absolutely none. The caves must also mark an evil, the privation of good, manifesting itself in sex (Aziz and Adela have been discussing marriage as they climb toward them). As to the assault in the cave, Forster eventually had the excellent idea of faking it by leaving everything about it in doubt.

There is a clue to the philosophy reflected in Marabar, and in the absence of Krishna from that road, in a letter written in March 1913 during Forster's first visit to Dewas, when he had 'a long talk about religion' with Bapu Sahib.

> He believes that we ... are part of God ... When I asked why we had any of us been severed from God he explained it by God becoming unconscious that we were parts of him, owing to his energy at some time being concentrated elsewhere. 'So,' he said, 'a man who is thinking of something else may become unconscious of the existence of his own hand for a time, and feel nothing when it is touched.' Salvation, then, is the thrill *we* feel when God again becomes conscious of us ...

Forster adds that the Rajah's philosophy is 'inspired by his belief in a being who, though omnipresent, is personal, and whom he calls Krishna'. But Krishna in *A Passage to India* seems to be neither personal nor omnipresent; in the caves he is totally absent, elsewhere he ignores supplication, yields to negativity; only in the last section of the book does he come and save, or enact salvation.

The significance of the presence or absence of Krishna in the pages of this novel is of course what no reader can miss, even if he or she has not even Godbole's dim understanding of presence and absence. Forster insists on his mnemonic rhythms – 'come, come, come'. We are not for a moment allowed to forget Krishna, absent or present – most of the time in the former condition, unwilling to come.

When David Lean wanted to make his film of this novel he had to persuade King's College to let him do it. He was very sure it would. There was a lunch given for him at which he ate nothing – I seem to remember that he did not even sit down. He wanted, needed, to dominate the table, and he did. He had already written and distributed the screenplay, and claimed that he knew the novel literally by heart. Challenged to test this claim by putting a question about the book that he might not be able to answer, I asked him to name Ronny Heaslop's servant (the one, you may remember, whom he calls for on his return from the horrible joy-ride on the Marabar road). Lean promptly said it was Antony; but Antony is Mrs Moore's unsatisfactory attendant, a Goan Christian who has nothing whatever to do with the case. The person Heaslop orders to come is called Krishna – in the manuscript, Arjuna: another alteration in the interests of emphasis on Forster's *petite phrase*. This Krishna also neglects to come – another piece of evidence that this novel calls for a more intent reading than the film gave evidence of.

The seed of the Krishna theme was sown when Forster was in Dewas with the Maharajah, who did puja to pictures of Krishna when distressed, and would ask, 'Oh, when will Krishna come and be my friend?' And there was the great absurd festival of the birth of Krishna, much of it devised by the Maharajah himself and celebrated with appropriate ecstasy. Forster transferred the Maharajah's interest in the god to Godbole, who, when Heaslop's coming has broken up Fielding's party, eventually and unexpectedly sings the milk-maid's song, in which Krishna refuses the girl's petition that he come not only to her but to everybody.

There are those who find the repeated invocation – 'come, come, come' – irritating. To one representative critic it is no more than a tiresome distraction from the business of the book. Andrew Shonfield, for instance, thought the entire Temple–Hindu section 'rather insubstantial, and in places positively banal' and described Godbole as 'that stock character, the Inscrutable Oriental'. He was especially annoyed by such episodes as Aziz calling to Mrs Moore in the mosque, 'Madam, madam, madam', but failed to relate it to the other occurrences of the little rhythm. He scolded the author for his rehandling of the story of the hyena or ghost (not understanding how deeply important the episode had become in Forster's imagination); for choosing a Moslem protagonist simply because he liked Moslems better than Hindus; and, in general, for his political failure. Where was the Congress party? Where Gandhi? Where the reformed native bureaucracy? And so on. Forster knew this kind of criticism well enough, and patiently repeated that the novel wasn't really about politics, though admitting that its political aspect was what made the book sell. What then was it about? He said it was 'about the search of the human race for a more lasting home, about the universe as embodied in the Indian earth and the Indian sky, about the horror lurking in the Marabar Cave and the release symbolized by the birth of Krishna'. Simple enough – not wholly satisfactory, but it helps to rule out the sort of interpretation which condemns the author for failing to analyse imperialism on the one hand and Hindu religion on the other. In a striking passage in the manuscript, later cancelled, Forster wrote of 'the larger disaster that has its roots outside humanity'. That may be the true subject; and it is certainly a large subject, another version of the aboriginal catastrophe.

Almost until the end it seems that Krishna, so often invoked, so obdurate, stubbornly refusing to come, is far from agreeing to multiply himself into a hundred Krishnas, as Godbole's milkmaiden requests. 'But He comes in some other song, I hope?' says Mrs Moore gently. 'Oh, no, He refuses to come,' repeats Godbole, perhaps not understanding the question. 'I say to Him, Come, come, come, come, come, come, come. He neglects to come.' Godbole has specified the *raga* he is using, which reminds us that the purpose of this passage is musical. Forster says he 'got the spiritual reverberation going' by means of a trick; 'but "voluntary surrender to infection" better expresses my state'.

An odd expression! Presumably the trick was to blur the account of the caves just as Miss Quested's skirt blurred the footprints of the beast. The source of the infection must be the caves, which are evil in the sense of signifying and promoting the absence of good, of thwarting attempts to provide some standing in the void for humanity, for mere being. The opposite of their *boum* is music, the music of the singers saluting the birth of the child Krishna in Dewas: 'I have no doubt I was listening to great art,' wrote Forster, 'it was so complicated and yet so passionate.' He thought art should be like that. To produce it required inspiration.

You could hardly call the caves his inspiration, though he comes near to doing so. Forster, as I've suggested, believed in inspiration in a quite matter-of-fact way. He got a little of it whenever he picked up a pen. As he explained, it does not necessarily produce good things, but it is a pleasing condition.

'The mind, as it were, turns turtle, sometimes with rapidity, and a hidden part of it comes to the top and controls the pen ... He [the artist] is not exactly "rapt"; on the contrary he feels more himself than usual, and lives in a state which he is convinced should be his normal one but isn't.' He enjoyed the feeling that what he was writing might be coming to him unbidden, even if it turned out to be no good. He recalled a poor story called 'The Rock' which came in that way. The initial 'given' might later be developed by a conscious process – by faking. He seems to have felt this way, receiving most from the unconscious, when writing *The Longest Journey*, 'the least popular of my five novels but the one I am most glad to have written. For in it I have managed to get nearer than elsewhere towards what was in my mind – or rather towards that junction of mind and art where the creative impulse sparks.' Like the Maharajah he evokes himself.

Though he believed fiction had no rules – 'there is no such thing as the art of fiction' – Forster was nevertheless devoted to the novel as a form of art requiring inspiration. He knew he could find this quality more easily, more brilliantly evident, in D.H. Lawrence, and he did not claim for himself the prophetic powers of that author. His experience suggests that his own brilliancies derive from a creativeness essentially more intermittent. The music comes from the placing of these intermittent discoveries and their inter-relations. The novel enshrines them in its prose, putting quasi-musical motifs within its realist structures. It is these moments, and not the 'elaborate apparatus' Forster deprecated, that are the means by which novels can be complicated and passionate. Writing *Passage* after his return from India proved to be hard work, but Proust helped him through it, providing an example of how inspiration can passionately complicate.

If you value art you will value the artist. This Forster did, including himself among the honoured group, though with those familiar self-deprecating gestures that muffle his certainty on the point. Creativity was a blessing but creative people were rare. He wanted to write books that would please creative people but be bought by all the others, those who might recoil from the complicated if not from the passionate. Where should he seek his readers? He considered 'Bloomsbury', a group of artists and intellectuals he knew well. 'Its contempt for the outsider plays a very small part in its activity, and rests on inattention rather than arrogance. Once convinced that he is not a figure of fun, it welcomes and studies him, but the rest of humanity remains in a background of screaming farce as before. Meanwhile the intellect – thinking and talking things out – goes steadily ahead ... Essentially *gentlefolks*, they would open other people's letters [Forster himself got into some trouble for doing so in India], but wouldn't steal, cheat, bully, slander or blackmail like many of their critics, and have acquired a culture in harmony with their social position. Hence their stability.' Forster contrasted them with the *gamins*, Joyce, Lawrence, Wyndham Lewis, and with the aristocracy 'who regard culture as an adventure and may at any moment burn their tapering fingers and drop it.' 'Academic background, independent income, Continental enthusiasms, sex talk ... They are in the English tradition. I don't belong automatically ... I couldn't go there for any sort of comfort or sympathy.' He admired Virginia Woolf but perhaps did not love her. He admired Cambridge but it depressed him: 'as soon as the train slackens at that eel-like platform it is settled who I can know, who not.' He liked the idea that God could be described, in Persian, as 'the Friend', for he valued friendship – also, perhaps, complicated and passionate – as he admired art. We recall that he claimed to have reached Islam via Hinduism. The Maharajah wanted

Krishna as a friend, but it is in Persian that the word can be used of God. 'I am not intimate with him,' wrote Forster of the Maharajah, 'and have never in my mind claimed intimacy. It is something else I am trying to say ... he remains one of the great spiritual experiences of my life.' Yet during his visit to India in 1945, when in his mid-sixties, he stopped his car to meditate in a ruined mosque, and, as his friends testified, often went down on his knees in mosques, like a believer.

The social discriminations outlined in that entry in the Commonplace Book are Arnoldian: barbarian aristocrats, solid Wilcox-like bourgeois; neither would do. And, as an ironical remark in *Howards End* informs us, the populace is unthinkable. Writing to Christopher Isherwood in 1933, he wondered whether he himself had not been more civilized thirty years earlier, when he had thought of himself as 'hiding a fatal secret', but then he denied it, saying that in truth he is now much more civilized, 'and so are we all, those good few of us who count.' 'Good few' – a sizeable minority? The few of us who are good? Plucky? Proud? Considerate?

Those words could serve as the text for a quite different lecture on Forster and his company of the plucky, the considerate and the proud, and of the other outcasts, and oddities, the gays, the artists – especially the great ones, the ones who have recognized their need to be interested in death, to accept the hostility of the universe; who have understood their fate, their election, and *mind* it.

I end with another word on ambiguous rhythms. At the end of *A Passage to India*, when Dr Aziz meets Ralph Moore and treats his bee-stings, but roughly, Ralph complains, 'We have done you no harm.' Aziz replies with feeling, ' "No, of course your great friend Miss Quested did me no harm at the Marabar." Drowning his last words, all the guns of the State went off ... Mixed and confused in their passage, rumours of salvation entered the Guest House.' Is this the end of Marabar, its boom drowned out by a festive salute?

Not much later Aziz and Fielding, now a fully committed Anglo-Indian, take a last ride together. It is a beautifully composed ending. They want to be friends, 'But the horses didn't want it – they swerved apart; and the earth didn't want it, sending up rocks through which riders must pass in single file.' The fists and fingers of the world, we may conclude, are still at work against friendship and love.

PART TWO

E.M. Forster: A *Causerie*

This second part differs in style and purpose from the fore-going chapters. After I had completed the lectures it seemed to me that there was good reason to look more extensively at Forster's life as an artist (the role he chose for himself) and to reflect not only on his creativity but on the personal and social circumstances that restricted it. I also welcomed the opportunity to write more about Forster and some other novelists who were his contemporaries or nearly so.

I have thought of this section of the book as a sort of *causerie*, a loosely organized sequence of observations ani-mated by a desire to achieve some understanding of a talent so considerable and yet so straitly limited. In pursuit of this aim I shall doubtless tread where many have trod before, and possibly test the patience of readers who may consider I have told them what they already know perfectly well, or that I have widened unduly the contexts in which I have tried to situate him; but the focus of Part One was narrow, and it seemed that there was some benefit to be had from allowing a greater breadth of reference in Part Two.

Between 1905, when he was twenty-six, and 1910, Forster's first four novels were published: *Where Angels Fear to Tread* (the first to appear, although not the first to be written), *The Longest Journey*, *A Room with a View*, and *Howards End*. So he could look back from the eminence of just over thirty and congratulate himself on an auspicious start. He published his last novel, *A Passage to India*, in 1924, when he was forty-five, and his reflections on fiction in *Aspects of the Novel* three years later. After that he lived on for forty-three years without publishing another novel, although he wrote an enormous amount of non-fiction – biographies, newspaper articles, lectures, broadcasts, journals, letters by the thousand, and a handful of homosexual short stories (published after his death). Leaving aside the posthumously published and inferior *Maurice*, one thinks of Forster primarily as the author of those five novels, a writer who began with confident originality, reached his apogee in 1924, and then stopped, much concerned about his loss of creativity but unable to recover it.

At the time of his death in 1970 he was still famous, perhaps more famous than he had ever been, though he sometimes found the fame a burden; he was, as his excellent biographer P.N. Furbank describes him, a quasi-sacred object of pilgrimage, rather like the Pope or the Pyramids. His life spanned the reigns of six British monarchs and he had been the contemporary of several distinct generations of novelists. Of his Cambridge contemporaries only Bertrand Russell outlived him, and his was a reputation of a quite different and more publicly assertive kind.

Certainly Forster's career had an unusual shape. His early achievements were exceptional, but when he died *Where Angels Fear to Tread* was sixty-five years old, deserving to be called Edwardian and, possibly, quaint, a collectible from the age when gentlemen might rush down railway platforms to procure footwarmers for travelling ladies. Conventions of sexual behaviour as observed in Forster's novels are so different from those of later fiction that two stolen kisses are sufficient to sustain the plot of *A Room with a View* and to give *Howards End* its cunning false start with the engagement that ends as soon as it begins, though with consequences that cannot be cancelled. What happens in *A Passage to India* to

Miss Quested in the cave, if anything does, is presumably more shocking than a kiss, but for all its skill that scene and its consequences belong to a world in which what may now seem fairly trivial sexual gestures carry a freight of irreversible significance. Instead of diminishing Forster's celebrity such archaisms seem, if anything, to have encouraged it, with some adventitious help from the films of his novels made by David Lean and by Merchant and Ivory.

Forster cared little for display, and if he was ever a little vain he confined his vanity to his private writings and the conversation of friends. As a dedicated homosexual he lived under threat from the law that ruined Oscar Wilde in 1895; he lived to see the enactment in 1967 of a more liberal statute that decriminalized hitherto forbidden acts between consenting adults, but he probably thought it came too late for him to allow publication of his 'gay' novel, *Maurice*, written in 1913 but published only posthumously in 1971.

Where Angels Fear to Tread, the first published work of an unknown beginner, seems to have had a generous reception. C.F.G. Masterman described it as 'original and masterly', and the *Spectator* called its author 'a writer to be reckoned with' though the book itself was 'disconcerting' and 'depressing'. These and other early reviews make it clear that Forster had, from the beginning, reasonably serious treatment, warmer than all but the luckiest of young novelists might expect today. The influential Masterman also gave *A Room with a View* a discerning notice, and he took another step in writing to Forster to affirm his pleasure in the book, though finding it to be 'irresponsible' – possibly a hint at moral looseness (those kisses) – for Edwardian reviewers were usually careful not to obscure the moral view. Some found *The Longest Journey* 'original' and 'amazingly clever', 'a novel to be noted', but also 'elusive', 'puzzling', 'incoherent'.

However, *A Room with a View*, as Philip Gardner remarks, enabled reviewers to admit Forster to 'the limited class of writers who stand apart from the manufacturers, conscientious or otherwise, of contemporary fiction'. And three years later *Howards End* – 'a general subject of talk in literary circles' – raised him, at a still very young age, to the company of the finest or best-regarded of contemporary practitioners. It remained for *A Passage to India*, the only one of his novels that cannot properly be called 'Edwardian', to acquire the status of a 'modern classic'. It did not escape criticism, some of it severe, as in condemnations of the trial scene – 'a serious blemish' and 'full of technical error'. Why hadn't Forster taken the trouble to find out how, and by whom, such trials were conducted? Indian reviewers were scathing on these points. A more general complaint was that the novel showed Anglo-Indians rather as they had been in the fairly recent past, with no concession to the prevailing view that their manners had recently become less offensive.

In the course of its largely favourable reception the reviewers showed little interest in almost any aspect of *A Passage to India* that has commanded the attention of dozens of more recent analysts and commentators. We are told that there is 'a queer kind of mystery connected with the Marabar caves' but that it 'is never cleared up'. This is a view of the caves, and of Miss Quested's experience in them, that Forster himself would later gloomily endorse: 'I tried to show that India is an unexplainable muddle by introducing an unexplained muddle – Miss Quested's experience in the cave. When asked what happened there *I don't know*'. Here one must be willing to say he was wrong, for in another mood he might have said he won the hard-fought struggle to deal with Miss Quested and the caves by means of the brilliantly ambiguous solution to which he eventually found his way. He had known in advance only that there would be a critical occurrence at Marabar. A mere kiss could carry serious symbolic weight but here would not be enough. In the end the right creative answer presented itself: something happened, perhaps nothing, or nothing much; yet it was catastrophic. If Forster, years after that struggle was over, was still looking for more plausible but unnecessary answers, one has to remember that the belated responses of authors to their own work can sometimes take forms of misprision or denial.

To go back to the beginning: Forster, working on the early versions of *A Room with a View*, was, as I've said, an obscure young man. He had no siblings and before his first birthday he had lost his father to tuberculosis. His mother, widowed at twenty-five, was left financially secure but emotionally demanding. In 1882 she leased Rooksnest, near Stevenage, the house on which the house called Howards End is modelled, and which both mother and son loved. But partly because of her indecision she failed to persuade its owners to renew the lease, and they began a new and not always happy career of house-hunting. Over the years there were difficult moments, but never a serious separation. Of the thousands of letters Forster wrote, a high proportion naturally went to his mother, and although he travelled a good deal and in his forties took a flat in London (in the Bloomsbury area) he shared her home until her death in 1945, when he was sixty-six.

At preparatory school he was unhappy in the usual manner of English boys, though, by a piece of luck few of them can hope to match, his aunt Marianne Thornton died when he was eight years old and left him in trust the sum of £8000, a large inheritance in the sterling of 1887. 'Her love,' said Forster in his biography of her, 'in a most tangible sense, followed me beyond the grave.' He certainly never experienced poverty; I suppose one could say that instead, by way of suffering, he experienced the deep, familiar unhappiness of life at an uncongenial public school. It left memories that colour the school scenes of *The Longest Journey* and the best chapter of *Maurice*.

Cambridge was another matter. There he worked at his Latin and Greek and history but also read widely. Academically sound but apparently not brilliant, he took second-class degrees in both the Classical and the History Tripos. Nevertheless, when one takes note of the reading he did outside these subjects (often noting it in his diary) and of the range of his post-graduate European touring, it is hard not to be impressed by his determination to learn. His college, King's, was well suited to a student with musical gifts, and these Forster certainly also possessed. He was at ease with his narrow circle of Cambridge friends, men who taught him something about the world, perhaps as much as it would be reasonable to expect in an all-male college. Elected to the celebrated and powerful society (or coterie, or club) known as the Apostles, he was philosophically devoted to the pursuit of truth, and made aware of the high value of personal relations and secular ethics. He said later that it was important for artists to belong to a clique but that they must take care to choose the right clique. He was able to do this, and out of King's and Trinity and the Apostles came Bloomsbury, a satisfactorily adult clique.

After Cambridge Forster spent an enviable year in Italy, not by any means an idle episode, enjoyed in conditions that would be thought almost luxurious by most modern travellers. This was not the grand tour of the previous century, but it was grand in its own way, suitably adapted to the high-bourgeois needs of his mother, who accompanied him throughout. Their travels were amply supported by the legacies of Mr Forster and Marianne Thornton, and conducted in line with the gentle but firm manners and studious aspirations of the Clapham Sect – for it was that noble and philanthropic group, founded in the early nineteenth century by William Wilberforce, Forster's great-grandfather the banker Henry Thornton, and others of like mind, that had established the ethics, the interests and the incomes of such minor descendants as E.M. Forster. Such were his advantages – not inconsiderable, and not wasted. It is not too much to claim that by his early twenties, and by the criteria prevailing for gentlemen a century ago, Forster was a very well-educated man. Later he entertained the idea that people of real creative power tended to be not very bright intellectually, and proposed Thomas Hardy (for whom he nevertheless claimed to have 'an idolatrous reverence') as an example. Lack of intelligence, he believed, could indeed be a sign of creative power, as in the cases of Michelangelo and Shakespeare. Goethe, he maintained, was the sole example of a being at once formidably creative *and* not stupid. This may not be wholly serious, something written in Forster's habitual epistolary manner. However, he was already sure that he himself was creative but he wanted to be intelligent and thoroughly well informed as well. He was also sure that it was in the writing of fiction that he could display his powers.

The letter about intellect and creativity I have just been citing was written in 1911, when he already had four novels to his name; but thereafter he faced a period of ill health and creative dryness during which he abandoned *Arctic Summer*, the novel on which he had been working. This was the result not of a lapse in intelligence or industry but of a decline in imaginative power.

The young Forster may have been privileged – he had money, influential friends, talent – but he still had to find his way into and through the Grub Street of his day if he wanted to be profitably published. Even positive evidence of creativity might not, in that competitive world, be enough to ensure acceptance without the intervention of agents or friends, capable of opening the doors of London publishers. Perhaps things were not as dismally bad as they were in the 1880s when George Gissing failed to flourish, but one still gets the impression that in the time of King Edward VII it was not much easier than it had been or than it would later become to cross those thresholds or to awake the favourable interest of editors and reviewers. It was necessary somehow to knock harder. Forster chose a career which, as there were many to tell him, required one to know the practical world of books, not just the writers but the publishers, the middle men, the opinion-formers. The archetypal figure who fitted all those trade descriptions was Edward Garnett. The young Forster's dealings with him were not prolonged or decisive, but they were important, and one should remember that his life was not wholly spent with Apostles and the denizens of Bloomsbury; publishing books required transactions in the market place.

The importance of Edward Garnett in the history of the modern English novel can hardly be overstated. He was born in 1868, the son of Richard Garnett, Keeper of Printed Books in the British Museum, in which institution he and his family were privileged to live. Richard Garnett was a cataloguer and bibliophile, polyglot and polymath, historian and reviewer. No young man could have asked for a more congenial literary background. Edward left school early and educated himself in London bookshops and the stalls, long since removed, in the Farringdon Road. Moving on, he worked in a publisher's office, ineptly wrapping parcels, but he rapidly acquired authority as a publishers' reader. In 1889 he married Constance Black, a Newnham College graduate seven years his senior and politically active as he was not; he became instead a friend of Yeats and other members of the Rhymers Club, mostly liberal-minded and mildly dissident companions from the intellectual underworld of those years. Constance, having learned Russian from refugees, became famous as the translator of Turgenev, Tolstoy, Dostoevsky, Chekhov and Gogol. Garnett wrote prefaces to her books and argued fervently for the superiority of the great Russians to all other practitioners.

Generous and, in his own sphere, powerful, Garnett owes his continuing fame to his dealings with the great novelists of the day, most of all for his support of Joseph Conrad, but he cared about good writing wherever he found it and gave priceless help even to unknown beginners. When the young Henry Yorke, still at Oxford and calling himself Henry Green, wrote the novel that became known as *Blindness*, Garnett worked with him on it as assiduously as he did with more senior figures like Ford Madox Ford and D.H. Lawrence. Later he commented critically on Green's second novel, *Living*, the strangeness of which baffled but did not shake him; he reviewed the book favourably in *The Observer*, clearly with no sense that it was slightly improper of him to do so. Thus Henry Green's career was launched. Of course it may have helped that Henry Yorke was rich and well connected; perhaps it was easier for him than for other gifted undergraduates to establish a useful relationship with a man like Garnett. But Yorke was also brilliant, and in unusual ways. Garnett, once interested, was conscious of a responsibility to a writer of high promise.

He read for several publishers, and one important benefit arising from his intimate knowledge of their world was that he had a good understanding of the gap between the tastes and demands of literary readers and those of the larger public on which the publishers depended most for their profits. That gap was a maddening source of worry to Conrad; he was a slow worker, usually in debt, and prone to regard publishers as voracious monsters. Garnett read his manuscripts and found him publishers. Conrad trusted him because despite his commercial connections Garnett was himself not without qualifications as an artist and knew what it meant to continue in that vocation while at the same time contriving to appeal to a public unconcerned with art. He would benevolently, and sometimes anonymously, oversee a book throughout its existence from sketches to published work. He could not offer life-saving loans to authors (as the agent J.B. Pinker sometimes did for the temporary easing of the financial agonies of the Conrads), but he did understood what was entailed in saving the novel as a serious form of art. The artist Conrad was Garnett's greatest success, but he was almost equally important to D.H. Lawrence, Dorothy Richardson and Arnold Bennett. He was a champion of the new and original, even when his defence of Arnold Bennett meant fighting a war with the likes of important 'bookmen' like Edmund Gosse and Andrew Lang. London was his parish and its publishers and editors were of his daily acquaintance. Typically, through his son David he established friendly relations with the newly important Bloomsbury group.

Forster was aware of Garnett's abilities and took note of his review of *Where Angels Fear to Tread* (an unsigned notice in the *Spectator*; the identity of the anonymous reviewer was apparently not difficult to discover). Forster commented on his 'flair' and also on his generosity and skill – Garnett, he said, picked up a novel by an unknown writer, 'forced an enthusiastic review into a magazine, and gave me a chance of reaching a public.' When *The Longest Journey* appeared in 1907 Garnett chose it as his 'Novel of the Week' in *The Nation*. In that novel there is a scene in which Agnes is urging her young husband, Rickie, a writer, to make his stories 'more obvious': reading them, her 'Uncle Willie floundered helplessly'. Garnett quoted this passage when he commented on *A Room with a View*, adding, 'it is not easy to explain the subtle quality of Mr Forster's brilliant novel to Uncle Willie and his kinsfolk'. To put it crudely, readers of that type weren't interested in art but only in a good read. Any recommendations as to conduct had to respect the prevailing bourgeois standards. Discriminating praise from a critic who had proved he understood the art of Conrad and of D.H. Lawrence gave Forster much pleasure at a time when, as he put it in a letter to Garnett, 'the Uncle Willies are encompassing me sorely'.

Forster now asked Garnett directly whether he could not 'cause it [*The Longest Journey*] to be reviewed' in an American journal, *The Nation*. Apparently this was beyond even Garnett's powers, but he managed to make favourable mention of *Where Angels Fear to Tread* and *A Room with a View* in a survey essay on English fiction he himself wrote for *The Nation*. He had already commended Forster's subtleties in print and would quite soon do so again, when *Howards End* appeared. It was pardonable, perhaps inevitable, that the young man, still encompassed by Uncle Willies but having this new access to literary power, would seek, like Conrad, Lawrence and Wells, to benefit from his acquaintance with Garnett. Forster did not like machinery, but he saw the advantage of having a master of the mechanics of publishing on his side. The passage in *The Longest Journey* in which Rickie has an interview with a London publisher may well draw on memories of a visit to Garnett's office.

What was the competition, whose were the big names among the novelists then, when Forster came to know Garnett? After *Jude the Obscure* (1896) Thomas Hardy had stopped writing fiction. Conrad's *Nostromo* (1904) and *The Secret Agent* (1907) were published on either side of *Where Angels Fear to*

Tread, and *Under Western Eyes* came out in 1911, just after *Howards End*. It is quite difficult to think of *The Secret Agent* as an exact contemporary of *A Room with a View*, yet it was so. Forster's novel has its little moment of terror, the consequences of which are a spiritual crisis and a happy ending. His poor are decorative but, as things turn out, impassioned Italian peasants, a murderer and his victim. Conrad's book, on the other hand, includes an attempt to blow up Greenwich Observatory and ends with an anarchist – 'frail, insignificant, shabby, miserable' – walking the drab byways of London carrying his bomb, 'a pest in the street full of men'. Here anarchism is a real threat, not an Italian romance. The world it threatens is the world in which Forster's novels, up to and including *Howards End*, all of which are entirely free of allusions to anarchism, were set.

It was already commonplace to call Conrad a great novelist, though the opinion was not reflected in sales; everything about him suggested that no lesser claim should be made. His ambition bore a certain resemblance to that of his anarchist professor: he was desperate and would take on the world. Or, surpassing his inadequate Mr Verloc, he would himself try to blow up an observatory situated at zero longitude, a barren symbol of the entire world. And Conrad writes extraordinarily dream-like scenes, like Verloc's uncanny summoning of the policeman in the park, that make one think of Dickens and Dostoevsky. Garnett, in another of his unsigned reviews, justly compared *Under Western Eyes* to novels by Dostoevsky and Turgenev, and that claim would in itself have entitled Conrad to a place on Forster's shelf, among those great Russian novels to which he thought all English contenders must concede their inferiority.

Yet Forster, who wrote so much and had so much to say about anything that interested him even a little, says almost nothing about Conrad. In *Aspects of the Novel* he complains rather obscurely about the voice of Conrad's narrator Marlow. In a review of Conrad's *Notes on Life and Letters* (1921), he writes that this partly autobiographical book shows Conrad to be 'misty in the middle as well as at the edges, that the secret casket of his genius contains a vapour rather than a jewel', which is itself vaporously obscure and does very little for the 'half-dozen great books' that he allows, in the same review, to Conrad. It seems that Conrad was not of much use to the young Forster, who was probably right in thinking that Garnett might be.

Another dominant figure of the time was Henry James, a friend of Conrad and like him a victim of the incomprehension of Uncle Willie. Forster's lack of enthusiasm for James as expressed in his study of the 'pattern' in *The Ambassadors*, only hints at his unwillingness to give James even a little sympathetic consideration. James's last three novels, by many thought to be his masterpieces, also appeared at this time, and the only one of them on which Forster spent more than a few unappreciative lines was *The Ambassadors*. But James comes up often enough in other writings by him: 'One can approach the meaning of pattern by seeing what James sacrificed to attain it ... snipping beetroots and spring onions for his salad; for I knew he would keep among the vegetables, if only because their reproductive organs are not prominent ...' 'Most of human life has to disappear – all fun, all rapid motion, carnality, etc. ... Maimed creatures can alone breathe in his pages ...' 'However hard you shake his sentences, no banality falls out ...' Forster accepted that James was a great man ('great' and 'greatness' being difficult words in Forster), but he seemed to have no regard for the aspects of novel-writing that interested James and expressly declined to follow the master's rules on 'point of view.' He even recommended James

to take a corrective course in Balzac as a tonic for his debili-
tation – Balzac, whom James so unstoppably, if not quite
uncritically, revered as 'the master of us all'. And some find it
strange that Forster should tease James for lacking 'carnality',
a matter in which James, despite his immense refinement,
rarely loses all interest. Indeed, with a small amount of adap-
tation the words of this critique might be applied by a hostile
adjudicator to Forster himself.

One of Garnett's less favoured protégés was John Galsworthy, also a friend of Conrad and eventually a recipient of
the Nobel Prize. Garnett gave full attention to Galsworthy's
text but was not very enthusiastic in his comments. Publishing,
his business, required the exercise of discrimination, and he
knew that Galsworthy would appeal to the taste of Uncle
Willie more than some of the other writers he favoured, like
Conrad. Galsworthy's best-known novel, *The Man of Property*, appeared in 1906 and inaugurated the Forsyte series that
Uncle Willie admired at the time (as did Uncle Willie's nephews
and nieces the television version). The first of his plays on
social themes, *The Silver Box*, also belongs to 1906.
Galsworthy, active in many good causes such as prison reform,
the divorce law and theatrical censorship, was as earnest as
he was successful.

Since Galsworthy and Forster had in common a middle-
class concern about middle-class attitudes to poverty, it would
be surprising if the younger author should have remained
quite impervious to the influence of the older man. And indeed
Forster, after abandoning *Arctic Summer*, warned himself
against 'the influence of Galsworthy, Wells, etc.', complaining
that he must avoid what he now regarded as a mistake in his
writing of *Howards End*, namely what he called 'trying to
look round civilization' – something he may have suspected
Galsworthy of doing. He felt he had been on the point of

repeating this mistake in *Arctic Summer.* His biographer P.N. Furbank thinks he abandoned that book because he needed scope for the more visionary side of his talent, and further suggests that Forster's first visit to India in 1912 was a timely corrective and an encouragement to that visionary interest. Perhaps so, but in one form or another the 'visionary side' was always alive; it had been dominant in *The Celestial Omnibus*, which came out (as a book) quite close in time to *Howards End*, and was active also in the stories collected posthumously in *The Life to Come.* Nothing about Forster is more mysterious than his conviction that those stories were his best work, the work he was born to write, unless it is the fact that T.E. Lawrence enthusiastically agreed with that judgement. At any rate it is unlikely that admirers of these stories would have much time for Galsworthy.

In his plays as well as his novels Galsworthy was at least a plausible plot-maker and an able craftsman (a description, as we may see later on, that would have struck Forster as insulting); and if he was also keen to 'look round civilization' he took the trouble to find out more about poverty than Forster ever did. For one reason or another, mostly perhaps by reaction from the ardent suffrage of several generations of Uncle Willies, his reputation has now faded. A product of Harrow and Oxford, he pitied the poor but understood the rich. As V.S. Pritchett remarked, he was a rebel against his own class, 'a gentleman amateur on the surface of social life', 'a moral toff'. This is a charge that might be brought against other writers of the period, including, on occasion, Forster, but there is a difference between the two as craftsmen. Forster's method – which he quite fiercely maintained was right, however different from Virginia Woolf's or, for that matter, D.H. Lawrence's – involves a sort of professional secrecy that sets him apart and demands from the reader a closeness of attention at first sight inconsistent with the more public, accessible aspects of his books, their placid and generally unsensational narrative movement. This was a kind of subtlety that Garnett appreciated, but he could hardly have assisted Forster as he did Galsworthy, whose manuscripts he worked on with an intensity of care that prompted Pritchett to call Galsworthy's response 'masochistic'.

When the representation of the poor is concerned, it is easier to talk of Gissing, who knew a great deal more of this subject, and at first hand, than either Galsworthy or Forster. But instead of feeling uneasy in their presence he positively hated them, even the educated ones who made a living in Grub Street. Pritchett justifies Gissing's attitude in terms that constitute the opposite of justification when applied to other novelists, especially of his period: 'To most English novelists, invigorated but narrowed by class consciousness, one class has always seemed comical to another; that is where Gissing is so un-English, a foreigner or an exile. He sees nothing comic in class. He writes as if it exists only as a pathos or frustration.' When Gissing looks around civilization he reports the misery of others and his own self-pity. There seems to be something about the very subject that disarms him, some disablement or some enfeebling infection caught from the subject itself. Forster once remarked that the virtue seems to go out of Conrad when he has to deal with women – a seminal loss. Perhaps poverty was in some cases similarly disabling.

Yet Gissing would probably not have had as much trouble with the character of Leonard Bast in *Howards End* as Forster himself did; he knew all he needed to know about 'board-school prigs' and the real or supposed tendency of the lower classes to steal the umbrellas of their betters. To a surprising extent one's attitude to *Howards End* depends, as I shall try to explain, on one's response to Bast. D.H. Lawrence thought

Forster's effort with Leonard was 'a brave try' – a generous comment, but Forster thought he had done better than that and was ready to say he was satisfied with his rendering of the domestic life of Bast and his mistress. It would no longer be easy to find admirers devoted enough to agree with him.

Howards End is still admired and still preferred by some critics to *A Passage to India*. Here I sympathize with Samuel Hynes, who was once of that opinion but later withdrew it, expressing some astonishment that he could ever have held it. Returning to it after a long absence, the reader may well be struck by features that distinguish it quite boldly from much contemporary fiction. It says a great deal about England, its landscapes and its roads (associated with the Wilcox's car and so doubly deplored), and – necessarily, given the story – it considers rather than adopts political positions. Margaret Schlegel can admit the existence of 'the abyss' of poverty at the level of destitution, and she can admit that six-hundred-pounds-a-year people have six-hundred-pounds-a-year thoughts. Wilcox can feel sure that his kind always have their hands on the ropes (a much-repeated trope, less obtrusive though also less pointed than the wisps of hay, the hay fever, and so on). More interesting is the debate in Chapter 15, the topic being 'How ought I to dispose of my money?' Although the characters admit that something must be done for the Basts of society, they believe it necessary to remember that 'the second generation had the right to profit by the self-denial of the first'. Some of them say the Basts will, after all, have the National Gallery, free libraries and tennis courts, only not money; others that only large sums of money can make a difference to the Bastian individual, it being for such a person 'the second most important thing in the world'. Would a Bast with money lose his soul? The discussion is comic but serious notions intrude. A small amount of money might pauperize the recipient, a large amount wouldn't. 'Money's educational ... [if not] distributed among the many in little driblets.' And so on. Only Mrs Wilcox, now dead, had the naive imaginative power or 'the more inward light' to understand possessions.

This is all lightly done, ironically uncommitted; though now and again one finds a straightforward political statement: 'I hope that for women ... "not to work" will soon become as shocking as "not to be married" was a hundred years ago.' When there is occasion to philosophize or moralize without irony or farce, the work of explanation is done by the author ('It is rather a moment when the commentator should step forward,' he says, and he does so when he wants to brood over the rights and wrongs of Mrs Wilcox's unexpected bequest; but he has already done so many times without that excuse.) Margaret Schlegel has a wide range of inexpert opinions, but they are qualified by her other attributes – liveliness, intelligence, amusement, femininity, sobriety – and when a more stable view of the world is needed she tries to provide it. But she is fallible, and then the commentator again has to come forward. *The Oxford Dictionary of Quotations* lists thirty-two passages from Forster, nine of which are from *Howards End*. It rarely matters who speaks these lines, and the most famous of them are clearly not attributable to the characters: 'Only connect' stands on the title page before there *are* any characters; 'telegrams and anger' belongs to Margaret; 'Death destroys a man: the idea of Death saves him' is also hers but is followed by a Forsterian disquisition on the subject of death (worthy to be placed beside that curious passage in *The Longest Journey* and other mortal musings I noted in my third chapter). In any case I must admit that my understanding of Margaret's wise saying is imperfect.

*

We must return to the matter of Leonard Bast and to the greater problem of poverty. There is a sense in which Forster's failure with the character of Bast – and his inability to recognize it as such – is the clearest indication of the failure to 'look round civilization'. This point is made with considerable force by Jonathan Rose in his book *The Intellectual Life of the British Working Classes* (2002), which includes a chapter entitled 'What was Leonard Bast really like?' Rose believes that a considerable element of the British working class in the early twentieth century – not only the growing number of clerks but miners and other tradesmen – was in fact quite well educated, by means of cheap books from libraries like the Everyman editions, cheap theatre tickets, and of course their own efforts, either at home or in their employers' time. Great readers, they were nevertheless confronted with the obstacle of Modernism. Rose accepts John Carey's thesis that Modernism was a means of asserting class superiority over 'mean suburban man', that the writers responsible for this attitude 'convinced themselves that the typical clerk was subhuman, machine-like, dead inside ...' and in this way sought to maintain their superiority in an age when educational opportunities were increasing. One sneer was to call the clerks 'half-educated', or products of 'the Board School', or, worse, 'a shiftless rabble'. Bast is what such people might have expected – uneasy among the rentiers, a vulgar pianist, his head 'filled with husks of books, culture – we want him to wash out his brain', as Margaret Schlegel says. The novel makes it clear that Forster regrets Bast's education and wishes he could revert to the admirable condition of the simple farm labourer. (Rose reminds us that Forster thought there was something to be said for the feudal ownership of land, and one might add that major difficulties in his own life arose from questions of land ownership.) Bast is removed from the story when, having been cheated out of his job by the whim of the rich Mr Wilcox, he is crushed by the collapse of a solid bourgeois bookcase. A Wilcox must, contrary to his bourgeois expectations, go to prison.

Despite the improbabilities of this denouement, the social structure stands firm. And yet, as Rose says, Bast represents a class not so intellectually impoverished as Forster makes him out to be, and he cites examples of young men in Bast's position who by their talents made their way into the middle class, taking with them an unaffected love for the classics with which they had begun their self-education. Among writers whom Rose lists as having begun life in much the same situation as Bast are Richard Church, V.S. Pritchett, Edwin Muir, Howard Spring, A.E. Coppard, and Neville Cardus – all at one time members of 'an office-boy intelligentsia', later to develop into heroic readers and writers. In terms of literary class, most were 'middlebrows' – the highbrow designation being reserved for 'Modernists'. Having transcended the condition of Bast, they might join the army of Uncle Willies, so carefully studied by Garnett, or they might find it possible to be more adventurous – for among them we find Muir, the first translator of Kafka (whom Forster nowhere so much as mentions), and Pritchett, probably the most resourceful English stylist of his age (who also eluded Forster's notice).

Among the humanitarian issues that had troubled his ancestors and would now trouble Forster's and other consciences (in an age becoming more aware of its problems), poverty was the most urgent, or at any rate it was suspected of being so. It was possible to be troubled by a failure to be deeply troubled by it. Two famous sentences in *Howards End* read: 'We are not concerned with the very poor. They are unthinkable, and only to be approached by the statistician or the poet.' The easy irony is sometimes missed. In a letter

written in July 1907, Forster counselled his great friend
Masood to be careful with the girls in Ghent, where Masood
was studying: 'If you want to feel sad, think about poverty;
that is interesting almost to madness if it grips you once.' To
make a success of Bast and represent not the poor of the 'abyss'
but the genteel squalor of the city-bound upper working class,
Forster needed to know that culture and to be careful with it.
And, as Lawrence saw, studying the matter from a different
social angle, Bast was the key to the whole book. There were
poor people in other of Forster's novels – Italian peasants,
shepherd boys – but here was a character that fitted into no
pastoral genre. Symbolized by an umbrella gone at the seams,
Bast was one of those 'who are obliged to pretend that they
are gentlefolk', and the writer had to show them in their
miserable homes or finding a way to react to the conversation
of educated and better-off young women as they responded
to music, to Ruskin, and so on. 'Bast' was not even the first
name Forster gave to this character, but the change introduced
an association with 'bastard'. He is described as having 'the
lilting step of the clerk'. What kind of gait is that? Does the
crowd that flows over London Bridge each morning 'lilt'? Is
this some handicap diagnosed exclusively in clerks and offering a physical image of a spiritual lack?

At least Leonard knows what has become of him and has
proved himself manly by his quixotic nocturnal walk. But the
fact is that Forster could not bear him or his wife, and made
sure they were pitiable, indeed repulsive. 'One guessed him as
the third generation, grandson to the shepherd or ploughboy
whom civilization had sucked into the town; as one of the
thousands who have lost the life of the body and failed to
reach the life of the spirit.' This sounds like the language of a
priggish curate. Margaret Schlegel, it seems, knows the type
very well and sneers at 'the vague aspirations, the mental

dishonesty, the familiarity with the outsides of books'. Society sends such messages to those who don't belong but persist in trying to. Bast commands some respect for trying, but he cannot acquire the social skills he imitates. Some kind hearts may pity him, but that is an error that can have disastrous consequences. It is base and vulgar of Bast to suspect Helen Schlegel of stealing his umbrella, but hers is a worse fault: she lets him into her house. His impregnating her is the next intrusion, the small-scale but shocking sack of a city.

Forster was probably incapable of providing a fairer account of Bast, for in general he saw the poor as different from 'us', unless they qualified as boys who might be available for sex or were Italian peasants or Indians, and he had no real understanding of them. Of course that goes also for women. Helen's account of her first meeting with Jacky Bast does neither of them credit ('I want my husband, what I have reason to believe is here') but it is Forster who stops the teasing and describes Jacky's arrival as a rising from the abyss, 'a faint smell, a goblin footfall', as if she had escaped from those evil passages in Beethoven's Fifth Symphony, and he finally identifies her as 'bestially stupid'. He offers as evidence for this characterization Jacky's grammatical errors, and in that respect she resembles Jane Austen's Lucy Steele, who gives herself away to Elinor Dashwood by using such expressions as 'my sister and me was often staying with my uncle' – which shows what it means to have been denied education, a point that Jane Austen, a favourite of Forster's, never tires of making.

Forster, not without misgivings as to the usefulness of the work, taught Latin at a Working Men's College in London, and he may well have observed instances of awkwardness and pretentiousness in his students; yet these were people who sought to 'better themselves' by acquiring at least an element of the learning and civility that he recognized as the birthright of a higher class. It is not a shameful ambition. Moreover they were many, thousands of them, some of whom must have been much less pathetic, sprightlier figures of a type congenial to Bennett and Wells – bright young men with no ambition to model their prose on Ruskin's or to sit down to a dinner of a 'soup-square' with a deplorable wife for company. The sordid scene that Forster sets in the Bast home – a scene with which he expresses his satisfaction – is persuasively wretched, but it makes no provision for other possibilities, for relationships between men and women of this class that were not so hopeless and so wretched.

It may seem strange that Edwardian writers, Forster among them, had such difficulty with the poor. It has been truly remarked that they are always with us, and novelists are supposed to have the skills necessary to the representation of persons. But it could be done only, it seems, with difficulty. One explanation supposes the novelists' mental separation of poverty from politics, their failure to see that poverty was a consequence of grossly unequal political arrangements from which the rich benefited and the poor did not. Alison Light's book *Mrs Woolf and the Servants* (2008) clearly expresses one aspect of the fixity of relations between employer and servant, often producing embarrassment in meetings even where there is good will or a show of it on both sides. Servants were paid badly, and the mistress's financial control of them extended into other parts of their lives – hence disciplinary severities, restrictions on free time, prohibition of 'followers'. There may have been, indeed there may be, a general inability to *imagine* society as other than a set of fixed and permanent arrangements, occasionally deplored but virtually immutable. Galsworthy called himself 'the least political of men' yet he cared about the poor and poverty as obviously a political phenomenon, though it may have required of the wealthy the wearing of a special, one might almost say innate, political armour to keep out the perception that it was so and to deny the consequences.

This ignorance was founded in a confidence that things were as they were with the same permanence as the laws of nature. As the contented poetess Cecil Frances Alexander put it in 1848, 'The rich man in his castle,/ The poor man at his gate,/ God made them high or lowly/ And ordered their estate'; words still sung by the children of rich and poor in the Sunday Schools of my era. William Godwin, in revolutionary time a half a century earlier than Alexander, wondered at the stability of the arrangements in the great houses of London, seeing in them a significant duality – with the rich, in their part of the house, living in great luxury (though complaining about the exiguous wages of servants) and the servants living in their part in prison-like squalor, compelled into dissipation and crime. Engels exposed the condition of the poor in Manchester, but eyes that could turn away from the London slums could contrive without too much difficulty to ignore Manchester. Galsworthy, somewhat later, had a political theory all his own: the upper classes only needed to be aware of their amazing luck to make the chances of revolution sink to zero. Such were the hopes of this kind novelist, who probably wasn't reading the novels of Arthur Morrison, a slightly older contemporary who wrote *The Hole in the Wall* and *Tales of Mean Streets* and other blood-curdling thrillers about the conduct of the scum of the earth in the East End; they could have best been regarded as tales of a ferocious but happily remote tribe. Attitudes like his required, even in gentle and intelligent people, adherence to a political principle that kept a man of property, even if he was also a man of principle, from taking a disinterested view of poverty.

There was no pressing occasion for Forster to have such a

view. Simple considerations of class forbade it. In a letter to John Lehmann in December 1940 he wrote: 'My difficulty with working class writers is that they don't make the working classes come alive – Leslie Halward is an exception, but as you imply he's not very important. They give *me* information and they give their comrades gratification. But that's all; gloom, indignation, aspiration in plenty, and plenty of stains on the tablecloth and coal-dust in the mine – but no living things to experience them ... Or to put it another way: I find that we middle-class do demand that people in fiction should seem to be alive, and that there may be a fiction I am not conditioned to appreciate, in which Ted at the table, Ed in the mine, and Bert at the works need not be differentiated. But I can't look at them in that way myself.'

Forster was not alone in finding workers uninteresting as characters and generally unsuitable for fiction as he understood it. I remember Angus Wilson, a humane man who admired Forster and was admired in return, more than once expressing, quite defiantly, a similar point of view. He shared Forster's interest in Jane Austen but praised Dickens with equal fervour; those characters in his own novels who belong to the upper middle class are sensitive, even if politely corrupt, and those from the lower orders tend to be criminal Dickensian types. And Forster's admiration for Lawrence was based more on the delicacies of *The White Peacock* than on his representation of the life and speech of miners.

It might be objected that despite the abundance of testimony he offers, Rose is wrong to endorse the charge made by John Carey. Forster never intended Bast to match the achievements of the 'office-boy intelligentsia' Rose has in mind. But that intelligentsia existed, a company of heroic readers and writers. Far from joining the ranks of the half-educated, far even from joining the middle-class army of Uncle Willies, they even read what their betters avoided – including politically subversive books and 'modernist' books like *Ulysses* and *The Trial*, the first of which Forster disliked, and the second of which (as I said before) he never mentioned.

Conrad is a name on which both modernists and their opponents made claims, with the author himself miserably hoping for more participation from the lowbrows and seeking Garnett's help to that end. When he finally succeeded in attracting a larger readership, it was with *Chance* (1913), a rather dull book of complicated structure that in its degree of difficulty might have been thought to deter an anti-Modernist public. But Rose's intelligentsia had adventurous tastes and perhaps would not accept the arguments made about them decades later by Carey and Rose.

The autodidacts also knew how to read Arnold Bennett and H.G. Wells, judging by the success of their books, and perhaps saw them as irrelevant to disputes about the modern and the anti-modern. Their work, though serious, was quite un-Conradian and very rarely suggestive of an affinity with Henry James.

Bennett was born in Hanley in the Potteries in 1867, a decade or so before Forster. His father was a solicitor without formal education, so his contemporaries would have placed him as upper working class. He was a very successful literary journalist before he wrote a series of novels set at least partly in the Potteries, the best, it seems to be agreed, being *The Old Wives' Tale* (1908). Wells was of a lower social standing; his father was an unsuccessful professional cricketer. His novel *Ann Veronica*, which appeared in 1909, just before *Howards End*, concerns a New Woman who goes to prison for taking part in a demonstration at the Houses of Parliament, not a fate one could imagine for Margaret Schlegel.

Wells, like Bennett, knew a lot about Modernism. He made

fun of Henry James and shunned his methods, but he understood them. Neither of these authors, who began life only a little better off than Bast, had any difficulty in situating themselves at the heart of contemporary fiction. Bennett spent some years in Paris and knew more about French fiction than most English writers, Henry James and Ford Madox Ford excepted. But James did not admire him, accusing him of sacrificing to 'fact' the more demanding responsibility of 'presentment', and of ignoring the demands of 'doing'. Bennett, for his part, thought *The Ambassadors* 'not quite worth the trouble of reading it'. James's revenge was taken in his essay of 1914 on 'The New Novel'. But Bennett, who at his best (as in *Riceyman Steps*) defied definition in terms of highbrow and lowbrow, congratulated himself, in the manner of James, on the skill of his own 'doing'. An important character in *Riceyman Steps*, a lowly but generous maidservant, so endeared herself to the public that Bennett obligingly extracted her from the novel and quickly wrote a novella in which she was the central figure. Like Wells, he had found for himself a very large public, and both men were amazingly productive in its service.

On the matter of 'doing', Forster was judicious. Concerned with technical problems that were private to himself, he made gentle jokes against James and, as I have already explained, sided with Wells in his dispute with the Master. This did not mean that he gave his unqualified approval to Wells or Bennett. He called *The Old Wives' Tale* 'memorable', remarking that its real hero was Time itself. His reservations did not concern the 'doing', though doing might well involve departure from a simple time sequence. Contemplating the careers of the two sisters, he observed that 'our daily life in time is exactly this business of getting old which clogs the arteries of Sophia and Constance, and the story ... cannot sincerely lead to any conclusion but the grave. It is an unsatisfactory conclusion.

Of course we grow old. But a great book must rest on something more than an "of course", and though *The Old Wives' Tale* is strong, sincere, sad, it misses greatness.' By writing the novel with a simple time-sequence – childhood to death – Bennett managed to be not tragic but merely sad.

There were good precedents for playing tricks with time – Forster mentioned works of Proust, Conrad, Sterne, Emily Brontë. (He might have added Ford Madox Ford, perhaps the best example at the time, but he didn't care for him.) What he would have thought of later modernist developments – distortion or defiance of time, the programmes of the *nouveau roman* and the sometimes illuminating musings of the narratologists – I cannot guess. But his appraisal of Bennett's novel is generous, allowing one to think it just missed greatness while leaving one to wonder how, except perhaps by studying Proust (or Ford), Bennett could have avoided mere sadness. He had chosen a sad tale, imagining that many readers are gratified by sad tales and may even prefer them to novels that are so 'done' that they become about themselves, rather than being about childhood, old age and death.

Howards End was a commercial success but not on the scale that Bennett's novels were, and not right away. Later paperback editions made Forster rich, but by then Leonard Bast was an archaism and intelligent office boys no longer sought to test their culture by conversation with people like the Schlegels.

Forster admitted that his interest in class developed rather late in his life, not unlike his delayed discovery of the 'facts of life', and presumably he means a *critical* interest. There were those who argued that in the first half of the twentieth century the novel as a genre was in bad shape, and that class had something to do with its decline. Forster agreed about the decline of the novel but was cautious about any signs of its recovery. Writing in 1941, when there was much talk about a hoped-for post-war revolution in education, and some evidence that the working class (now mostly in uniform) could produce authors of talent who could satisfy any existing demand for verisimilar renderings of life in the mine and the pub, Forster did not welcome this news, perhaps because he was already tired of being *informed* about that world and instead wished, vainly, to be *gratified* by these new authors.

Yet there were those who thought there was a need for novels to describe, perhaps even account for, the condition of the poor, to reflect the growing sense of a social crisis in which the poor were deeply involved. This was all the more urgent in the midst of the war. Official reports and statistics supported such worries and perhaps even increased the widely shared sense of fore-boding, indefinite but menacing. The idea that the novel, of all forms of art, should be the one most capable of direct rep-resentation of social conditions seemed (and still seems) to many people obvious; at some point politics will intrude into novels that honestly achieve some effect close to that.

In the 1930s, many novels were written expressing a 'pro-letarian view' of the economics and politics of the day: of poverty, unemployment, the Spanish Civil War, the threat of fascism. A competent survey of these books may be found in Andy Croft's *Red Letter Days* (1990). Yet Croft does not cite the writers whose names are in any degree familiar to us, nor the works of the miner Lewis Jones and his like (whom I discussed in my *History and Value*), nor the books by an experimental middle-class Marxist like Edward Upward. Rather, he mentions Christopher Isherwood and Cecil Day Lewis and others who were considered to have eventually 'betrayed' the working class. Not one of the hundreds of books strongly favouring the Left that he lists is famous as a portrait of its times and of its class conflicts; there is nothing in the least resembling Steinbeck's *The Grapes of Wrath*, unless we count Upward's rather heroic trilogy and, in a quite different register, George Orwell's early fiction. It is as if taking an interest in such proletarian books required a prior political decision. This might reflect the opinion, now often expressed on the left, that a public school education was a disabling inheritance, notoriously so among poets but also among prose writers – hence the dilemma of Orwell, mistrusted on both sides, old Etonian and down-and-out.

Forster was not blind to the world; he had witnessed hunger marches, he had watched the City burning, and his close friend the policeman Bob Buckingham, whose job took him nightly into the bombed streets of London, described for him the ordeal of the poor during the Blitz. He read widely, if not systematically, and seriously but cautiously praised Christopher Caudwell's Marxist books (though 'no one who reads them will feel that a Communist makes a comfortable neighbour') despite their assault on bourgeois mythologies and their advocacy of proletarian culture. But it was almost as impossible for him to be interested in Communism as it was for him to care for Oswald Mosley. What he hated was violence and gross infringements of personal liberty; his reaction to the two upper-class names was characteristically liberal – Caudwell (Christopher St John Sprigge was his real name) must be allowed his say, but Mosley was the enemy of everything that liberalism, already losing its struggle to exist, stood for.

By the late 1930s Forster was lamenting the sacrifice of personal relations to new and destructive forces – speed being one, the need for concerted political action another. Great changes in the general culture were combining to end old-style liberalism and its cult of the individual. The novel, indeed literature more generally, might well be among the casualties. In 1937 he wrote,

> No serious person has the time to be a great writer. The serious
> person produces propaganda, party pamphlets, not what we
> were accustomed to call 'Works of Art' ... I very much doubt
> whether the particular form of literature which has interested
> me, mainly [namely?] the novel, is likely to survive. The novel
> has always been the stronghold of individualism: it expresses
> the writer's outlook, it deals with characters and the relation
> between them; it makes a great fuss over love affairs and social
> nuances. I don't think people will have the patience to write
> that sort of thing any more, even if they have the time.

The novel could still make a fuss over love affairs, but the
evidence of the 1930s and 1940s lent little support to the view
that it had been helpful in understanding the Condition of
England. In a sense it could be said that the poor, who would
need to be taken into account, remained as invisible to the
rich as they had been in the time of Henry Mayhew, who in the
mid-nineteenth century revealed for a moment the condition of
London 'street folk'. He was not writing fiction but was
describing forms of life to which he and a few other journalists
saw a need to draw attention. He could be compared with an
anthropologist reporting a formerly unknown tribe. He noted
that the jaws and cheekbones of his subjects were more developed. He observed a repugnance to 'regular and continuous
labour, a want of providence in laying up a store for the future'.
He detected a passion for 'stupefying herbs' and fermented
liquors, an insensibility to pain and an immoderate passion
for gaming, a passion for 'libidinous dances' and for war. Add
to all this immoderate and dangerous behaviour a desire for
revenge, a weak understanding of the nature of property, an
indifference to chastity in women, and a very vague sense of

religion, and you have a serviceable account of one class of poor people, 'street folk'. He thought of them as nomads, belonging to no settled city, though somehow related to the industrial workers who, driven out of the country, now, as best they could, occupied London.

Walking north from Covent Garden I have often found myself recalling some words of Thackeray, written in shocked response to Mayhew's famous series of investigative articles published in the *Morning Chronicle* in 1850: 'a picture of human life so wonderful, so awful, so piteous and pathetic, so exciting and terrible, that readers of romances own they never read anything like to it ... Yes; and these wonders and terrors have been lying by your door and mine ever since we had a door of our own. We had but to go a hundred yards off and see for ourselves, but we never did ... We are of the upper classes; we have had hitherto no community with the poor. We never speak a word to the servant who waits on us for twenty years.' Thackeray, like many other gentlemen – authors and publishers and lawyers – was a member of the Garrick Club, from which the district known as Seven Dials, one of London's most horrifying slums, was not much more than five minutes' walk away, but in a direction not often taken. For Forster's generation 1850 was not so long ago that Mayhew had become irrelevant. The first wife of Leslie Stephen, father of Virginia Woolf and Vanessa Bell, was Thackeray's daughter. There is a discernible connection between Thackeray's momentary self-reproach in the Garrick and the consciences of intellectuals in the 1930s, another ten or fifteen minutes up the road in Bloomsbury.

It remains a problem that although Forster read a lot, he failed to concern himself with works that others believed or now believe to be of special interest and importance. Of course he was under no compulsion or necessity to do so, but since he produced so much journalism – reviews, broadcasts, columns here and there – and was for a while the literary editor of the *Daily Herald* in London, one perhaps unreasonably supposes he might have sought out the big ones. But he seems not to have read anything by Graham Greene or Henry Green, by V.S. Naipaul or V.S. Pritchett, by Anthony Powell or Muriel Spark. He read French and Italian well; he knew his Proust but not his Camus. I don't think he so much as mentions Thomas Mann, or Robert Musil, any more than Kafka. He was acquainted with Steinbeck and Dos Passos and is known to have read *Lolita*.

He evidently did not make much attempt to read systematically, except when he was preparing for some special event or series, such as the Clark Lectures. Search for his opinion of, say, Ford Madox Ford and you find nothing more interesting than the epithet 'fly-blown', while the highly original and productive writer, painter and controversialist Wyndham Lewis he dismissed as a 'sulky tinker' – these of course being social and not aesthetic valuations.

We also do not have record of his views on a major dispute that began in 1917 with Virginia Woolf's persistent and occasionally impolite attack on Arnold Bennett, and became one of those important literary quarrels in which the disagreements of the participants deepen with every shot fired until they bring to light cultural differences more profound than the ones they began by advertising. Such were the battles between the Ancients and the Moderns fought out in the late seventeenth and eighteenth centuries, in both France and England – best remembered in England because of Swift's essay *The Battle of the Books* (1697) but more fierce and pedantic in France. The Bennett–Woolf encounter lacked the fierce commitment of this old argument, but it was not without resonance.

In 1917 Bennett was the most successful of living British

novelists and Woolf the author of only one novel, *The Voyage Out*, a *succès d'estime* but not a commercial triumph in the Bennett manner. She attacked Bennett as an 'Edwardian', allowed herself to note his relatively humble social origins and questioned his power to create character. A more sustained attack followed in various essays, notably the well-known 'Mr Bennett and Mrs Brown'. Bennett replied, rejecting the charge that he couldn't do character and suggesting that on the contrary it was his opponent who couldn't, in support of which charge he cited *Mrs Dalloway*. Samuel Hynes, in his excellent account of the dispute, defends Bennett against criticisms that have been made of this response, and shows them to be wrong on important points. To say, as Woolf did, that 'character had changed' recently due to various causes – including the exhibition of French Post-Impressionists imported from Paris in 1910–11 by Woolf's friend Roger Fry, and the delayed availability of *The Brothers Karamazov* (now finally in English, thanks to Constance Garnett) – was probably true, but Bennett had read Dostoevsky's novel in French before Garnett's English version appeared, and he was at least as familiar with its revolutionary power as Woolf was. His taste in fiction and in art was exceptionally refined, though evidently not the *echt* Bloomsbury level of refinement, and if she chose to think him lowbrow he accepted the description for the sake of argument: he was Life and she was Art.

The contention was not fairly fought and not very impressive or productive. Woolf's best, most characteristic work lay in the future, and neither disputant gave credit where it was due. It was almost a personal matter: 'One waited for her to snap', Forster said. Yet these sometimes petulant disagreements have this in common with the Quarrel of Ancients and Moderns: they were symptomatic of a sense of crisis, and they suggested that all parties' response to the past had changed. Some things, once acceptable and admired, would no longer do; such was Bennett's view of Galsworthy, for example. Some topics that had been considered in isolation from one another were now felt to be obscurely related: the Condition of England, the fragility of the Empire, the matter of the poor and the matter of class. What was the modern condition of the novel and its characters? What was Uncle Willie's view, and what were his demands? Would he accept that novels had in future to be aware that, as James proposed, every novel is dual, being about itself as well as its ostensible topic?

Quite soon there would be Joyce's *Ulysses* to consider (and reject) and *Portrait of the Artist as a Young Man* was already available. Was it not rather scary? What was one to make of *Tarr* (1918), the extraordinary novel written by Wyndham Lewis – painter, satirist, pamphleteer and leader of the dissident art movement Vortex? What of the avant-garde, of the groups, cliques, coteries, of the invading Americans (Pound, Eliot), of the newly received Russians and the Ballets Russes, of the religions of the East, or even of the home-grown Fabians and combative women's movements? To some it appeared that changed social conditions required changed allegiances. Some demands were utopian, some authoritarian. And one had not yet quite come to terms with Darwin or Einstein, whose Special Theory of Relativity, published in 1905, was almost as old as heavier-than-air flight, older than *Howards End*, though not as old as telegrams and anger. Forster took no part in the Woolf–Bennett exchanges: though he probably had a good deal to say on either side he was constitutionally averse to exhibitions of that kind, and anyway might have preferred not to say as much as his conscience required in favour of Bennett.

Forster both liked and disliked what he called 'the seclusion of colleges'. When in 1946 he was made an Honorary Fellow of King's College and, as an unusual favour, invited to reside in College, he was glad to be back, permanently, in the university where, as an undergraduate, he had been accepted into an élite. Yet sometimes he was impatient, needing a larger world. He complained in a letter to Virginia Woolf in 1927, long before he took up residence, that the college was 'a dirty place, always washing one's hands. And bad complicated food.' But he was conscious of the honour done to him, liked to entertain undergraduates, and was on amiable terms with his colleagues. Still, in his last illness he chose to be cared for not in the seclusion of King's but by his friends the Buckinghams, in whose house he died.

Fatherless and brought up or, as some said, 'coddled' by women, he had felt not at all at home as a student in a second-rate public school but very much so as a young man at King's and among the Apostles, chosen to be among the chosen. So after 1946 he was, on his own terms, at home. Yet more than once he expressed a mild dislike for Cambridge. It was part of his character that he enjoyed the companionship, sometimes sexual, of men whose appeal sometimes depended on their being alien to his class, men whom he certainly could not entertain at his college. He wanted class to disappear, but, as his Cambridge contemporary L.H. Myers, the son of a famous don and himself an ambitious novelist, remarked, 'class cuts down to the bone. It can be transcended, but not annihilated, in personal relationships.' Myers perhaps transcended the barriers of class by forming a relationship with the Communist party, but the barriers did not fall down. (Incidentally, he was part-owner of the celebrated London restaurant Boulestin's. Here is something instructive about British arts and politics of the 1930s: highbrow novels, principally with exotic Indian themes, admired by F.R. Leavis and Downing College but not by Bloomsbury and King's, written by the son of the founder of the Society for Psychical Research, a rich Communist owner of a restaurant famous long after his books were forgotten.)

In some respects Forster achieved the transcendence of those barriers, yet he, like most of his friends, was incurably of his class, even though he wished that he and his friends could be free of it. He needed servants and thought it *natural* to have them. (That, I think, is the real test: whether one accepts servants as aspects of the universe one has been born into and not merely as benefits to be purchased or hired.) May Buckingham, a close friend despite her sex and her marriage to the policeman Forster loved, thought (in the friendliest way) that Forster was a demanding guest; he dropped his clothes on the floor when he went to bed, sure that someone else would pick them up and deal with them. For him it was natural that matters should be so ordered; to pick up the clothes oneself might be a false or improper politeness.

Forster was conscious of, though modest about, his own social distinction, for he had grand ancestors of high bourgeois stock. Now and again he would sound a note of contempt for members of his own upper-middle class, and he particularly admired men who easily escaped that category – T.E. Lawrence, notably, but also, with the evidence of distinction being of a different sort, D.H. Lawrence and Edward Carpenter. When he had a long and occasionally bitter struggle with an aristocratic landlord, he reminded himself that he too had grand connections. He saw himself as 'a historic figure, if not a very important one; the last survivor, the last possessor of a particular tradition', and he described his Commonplace Book entries as the 'last utterances of the civilized'.

There must have been something about the way he talked that supported that impression. He could be a bit of a snob when writing to his mother, and he noticed with interest that it was possible for a servant, though of long standing, to dislike her. In his world servants were loyal but also maddeningly perverse and stupid; one treated them considerately as if they were of the same substance as oneself, or fought with them in a manner to which they, not oneself, were accustomed. Margaret Schlegel, in *Howards End*, reminds herself of her duty 'to remember the submerged' but is upset not by their plight but by the failure of an expedition to hire servants. And another passage in that novel raises a fence at which even the equable Furbank refuses:

> Perhaps the keenest happiness he [Leonard] had ever known was during a railway journey to Cambridge, where a decent-mannered undergraduate had spoken to him. They had got into conversation, and gradually Leonard flung reticence aside, told some of his domestic troubles and hinted at the rest. The undergraduate, supposing they could start a friendship, asked him to 'coffee after hall', which he accepted, but afterwards grew shy, and took care not to stir from the commercial hotel where he lodged.

D.H. Lawrence rather oddly described Forster as 'the last Englishman' – and, as we've seen, Forster was inclined to think of himself in the same way – but in 1910 there must have been plenty of such Englishmen around, not quite knowing what to do or say about the likes of Leonard Bast, whether to be pleasant like the Schlegels or homicidal like the Wilcoxes.

Yet it would be absurd to think of Forster as exclusively self-involved or clumsy in his social dealings. True, he was inclined to severity of judgement – to be so was somehow the responsibility of one who regarded himself as 'the last little flower of a vanishing civilization' – and I am told by Lady Spender, who knew him quite well, that the first epithet that came to her mind when she thought of Forster was 'censorious'. He wanted to keep you up to the mark, having standards of behaviour with which he was certain others ought to conform, and we find him scolding not only his dear friend Masood but also D.H. Lawrence and Benjamin Britten, which is impressive, since neither was known to be a ready turner of the other cheek. He was capable of writing a sharp reproof when friends left him out of their annual excursion to the Thames to watch the Boat Race.

He read and wrote a great deal and spent many hours at his piano; but to think of him as sedentary and leisurely or, to use his word, 'loitering' would also be absurd. For a man of his period he had travelled a great deal, not only in India, and he was very good at settling into strange environments and jobs, as he did during his time as a tutor in Germany, later in Alexandria and most of all in India. As time went by he became much richer than he needed or wanted to be, and although he acknowledged the presence of money as if it were permanently in the background of the kind of life he preferred, he was generous to his friends and occasionally to others. He really was ethically distinguished, doing good without fuss, true to himself rather than to an inherited Christianity.

He had some working-class friends and was not distressed by their relative lack of education. Writing in 1941, when, as I have mentioned, there was much anxious talk of a post-war revolution in education, and some evidence, which Forster found tedious, that the working class could produce writers who had talent and could show the world the life of the mine and the pub. John Lehmann, though about as far from being working class as anybody could be, tried as an editor to justify those hopes. *Penguin New Writing*, with its contributions from soldiers, airmen, miners, folded in 1950, and most of them found less interesting civilian occupations. At the end of the war Forster had most wanted the restoration of England's lanes and fields, of a just, old-style England without the old cruelties and hatreds – a liberal England, devoted to liberty and self-expression. The divergence between these hopes and the aspirations of the veterans of 1945 grew very wide. It was difficult for the middle classes to understand the result of the 1945 General Election. I was on a ship in the Pacific when that happened and I remember the incredulity with which regular officers heard the news of the Labour landslide; only I was content.

We have our trusted formulas for understanding the Edwardian Age and solve some historical problems by extending it to 1914. Forster saw it all and had only reached his mid-thirties when it ended. He was well placed to observe the change of character to which Virginia Woolf, in that famous phrase, assigned the date of December 1910, and to observe the social tensions we identify as peculiar to the Edwardian Age. The old guard was still Victorian, but protest against various forms of oppression – in politics national and international, in religion, in sexual conduct – was growing and sometimes becoming violent. On the workers' side militancy was replacing docility; there was more of it in the Women's Movement, and everywhere uncertainty where there had been confidence. Some of these doubts related to national and imperial security.

The Germans were building battleships in frightening numbers and aggressive design; they belonged to a new age of technology just as surely as telegrams and motor cars, and they stood for anger on an international scale. Fear of their intentions could be transferred to the dangerous and symbolic possessions of the Wilcoxes and their kind. They might well be upset by their newspapers, for the news of empire was not good. The British, having got away with a victory in South

Africa, faced the German threat with no obvious allies, and must themselves build very expensive dreadnoughts. Reports on the medical examinations of young men, needed for soldiering, showed all too persuasively that the health of the lower classes was bad and getting worse. It seemed probable that they were suffering the consequences of a diminution of well-being, and probably happiness, caused by the great nineteenth-century migration from country to town; yet the poor were regularly blamed for their own misfortunes and privations, and the response of the ruling class to their behaviour grew less and less clement or indeed reasonable. The workhouse, the orphanage and the dispensary were firmly associated with rigorous discipline. (But the palliative of the old-age pension arrived in 1909.)

When Forster lamented the motor car, deplored early aviation, and repeatedly complained that he belonged to a former age, he was awkwardly placed. Commentators complained of, or in some cases gloried in, the splendid isolation of England, but at least until 1914 access to Paris and beyond it Europe was very easy – a sovereign bought a ticket at Victoria and there was no trouble about passports – and Forster, as I've said, was a willing traveller. It was not intellectual privation he suffered; he spoke good French and Italian and some German, he found friends to accompany him on many cross-Channel trips, and he met European writers – indeed, in his later years, when he had become a conspicuous public figure, a great many of them. The old, late-Victorian avant-garde had used Paris as a second home for years. One could aspire to acceptance at Mallarmé's Tuesdays and the pleasures of Parisian nightlife. It was in Paris on the threshold of the new era that Yeats saw *Ubu Roi* and made his apocalyptic comment: 'After us, the savage God.' He meant 'after Mallarmé and Villiers de l'Isle Adam, after Gustave Moreau, after Jarry', after himself.

Later, after 1914, the words of Yeats came to sound less figurative. On 4 August 1914, Henry James wrote to Edward Emerson words even more memorable than those of Yeats:

> It has all come as by the leap of some awful monster out of his lair – he is *upon* us, he is upon *all* of us here, before we have had time to turn round. It fills me with anguish & dismay & makes me ask myself if *this* is what I have grown old for, if this is what all the ostensibly or comparatively serene, all the supposedly *bettering* past, of our century, has meant & led up to. It gives away everything one has believed in and lived for – and I envy those of our generation who haven't lived on for it.

In this and other letters James announced the end of an epoch in terms that Forster would surely have accepted.

A more pacific notification that an epoch had ended was the Post-Impressionist exhibition (1910–11), imported from Paris by Roger Fry. Forster attended the private view but found Gauguin and Van Gogh 'too much for him'. In so saying he joined the majority of those who visited the show. Arnold Bennett, however, despite his humble origin, had learnt something in Paris, and knew enough about the matter to review the show with understanding. Some, including Fry's close friend Mrs Woolf, might have expected to find Bennett on the philistine side; but as his sympathy for the Post-Impressionists shows, he was closer to the avant-garde, to the modern, to what we might even call the Bloomsbury club than Forster, though he stuck to his own line when it diverged from theirs.

Forster, as I've said, believed in clubs and cliques, and he enjoyed them; he was a member of the Reform Club, where he often dined with his guests, also of the Savile, then a favoured resort of writers. He also belonged to the 1917 Club, the Memoir Club, the Oxford & Cambridge Music Club, which had rooms in Leicester Square and thus was conveniently placed for the opera. In a sense he could be said to have made his choices early, since as an undergraduate he'd thought of King's as well provided with clubbable people, and the Apostles were, after all, a famous and powerful club, but London offered more choice. Commonplace religious observance (in any case fissile) was spawning sects under the pressure of Darwinism and the newly advertised Hindu religions. Even the severely rational Fabian Society, a political and scientific party, had inherited a small mystical streak. William Butler Yeats, while in London, involved himself in all manner of business relative to the Order of the Golden Dawn, to the operations of Mme Blavatsky, and to various Irish secret societies. Forster seems to have kept out of organizations of that sort, though the Memoir Club, a rather cliquish and somewhat quakerish Bloomsbury sect, had a certain tone: its members swore to read to one another their absolutely true memoirs – surely an impossibly severe qualification.

Forster also wanted a different kind of association. There seemed to be no limit to his desire for the company of gifted young men. In the 1930s he counted among his younger friends W.H. Auden and Christopher Isherwood, and even after they left for America in 1939, they did not forget him – he makes vivid appearances in Isherwood's autobiographical writings. In *Down There on a Visit* (1962), Isherwood wrote, '[Forster is] immensely, superhumanly strong. He's strong because he doesn't try to be a stiff-lipped stoic like the rest of us, and so he'll never crack. He's absolutely flexible. He lives by love, not by will . . . His silliness is beautiful because it expresses love and is the reverse side of his passionate minding about things . . . we need E.M.'s silliness more than ever now. It gives courage.'

That passage alluded to a lunch the two men had had together in the autumn of 1938, at the time of the Munich crisis, and 'silliness' is a Bloomsbury expression. Leonard Woolf, reflecting on the importance to the national life of 'an intellectual aristocracy of the middle class', had written of the tradition of tolerance cherished by its members, and he identified as a product of that tradition the kind of person he called a 'silly'. He may have been thinking of the old sense of the word, 'simple' or perhaps even 'saintly', and he claimed 'there was something of the "silly" in Virginia ... and there was a streak of the "silly" in [G.E.] Moore and in Forster'. One may suppose that silliness was not always charming. In a letter to Lytton Strachey, Woolf described an occasion in 1904 when he and Forster found themselves in Green Park 'surrounded by board school children and workmen on their faces [?]; he was just as querulous and apologetic as usual' – evidently not sounding at all silly. It is helpful to set beside Isherwood's excited words the colder but still friendly appraisal in Virginia Woolf's Diary for September 1922, when she already knew Forster well (and he admired her perhaps a little more than she admired him): 'I am impressed by his complete modesty (founded perhaps on considerable self-assurance). Compliments barely touch him. He is happy in his novel, but does not want to discuss it. [This was *A Passage to India*, and he was not very happy about it.] There is something too simple about him – for a writer, perhaps, mystic, silly, but with a child's insight: oh yes, & something manly and definite.' At the precise moment when she was writing these notes, and in the same room, Forster was in conversation with T.S. Eliot, who was asking him to write for his journal *The Criterion* – two sillies and one man of sense.

P.N. Furbank, describing his own first impression of Forster, noted 'his fine eyes, in steel-rimmed glasses, and a most expressive and sensitive mouth, by turns tremulous, amused, morally reproving or full of scorn. It was the mouth, one felt, of a man defending the right to be sensitive. Physically he was awkward, limp and stiff at the same time.' Furbank goes on to describe certain graceful gestures, whether signifying a blessing or just the manipulation of a teacup. His brilliant portrait sketch seems in harmony with the views of the Woolfs and with the character of the 'silly'. Yet that mischievous observation of Percy Lubbock's – based, after all, on long acquaintance – may be fair enough: 'It's really too funny your becoming the holy man of letters. You're really a spiteful old thing. Why haven't people found you out, and run you down?' Forster replied cheerfully: 'They're beginning.'

Some of the Bloomsbury people were a little afraid of Eliot, for he was sometimes a rather severe presence, but Forster seems not to have been. He saw a good deal of Eliot and admired him for his influence as well as his poetry (though disliking his 'reverence for pain'). He even seems to have entered into silent competition with Eliot, confiding to himself, late in his life, that he was 'as far ahead of [Eliot] as I was once behind'. I imagine he meant 'ethically', as it would be odd to make the novels of one and the verse of the other the subjects of a competition. But it is easy enough to believe that Forster wasn't afraid of this very authoritative figure. He was, in Virginia Woolf's special sense of the word, 'manly'. He had bouts of rage, sometimes lost control of himself and threw the furniture about, but he was capable also of 'simulated benignity' when the occasion required it, as Furbank observes. Moreover the whimsy, the humour and the easy flow of his critical writings, as well as what might be called their lack of critical analysis, do not conceal his high standards.

Forster was an artist, and made a sharp distinction between what was art and what was not. Of his collection of miscellaneous essays *Abinger Harvest*, he said it was 'imperfect when compared with real writing'. More than most artists, he was willing to look back over his earlier works to discover and discuss their faults. *The Longest Journey*, which he thought should have been the best of his novels, had gone wrong, he thought. 'I am amazed and exasperated at the way in which I *insisted* on doing things wrong there. It wasn't incompetence; it was a perversity the origins of which I can no longer trace ... The L.J. has never stopped working in my mind ...' He expressed this view in a letter to Peter Burra, a young critic Forster admired for the sensitivity and understanding he showed in an essay that Forster later chose to be used as an introduction to the 1942 Everyman edition of *A Passage to India*. Forster thanked Burra for noticing that the prose of *The Longest Journey* 'heightened' before the entrance of Stephen Wonham, and later, in explaining why he had chosen Burra's essay: 'Burra saw exactly what I was trying to do.' Coming from Forster, who claimed that criticism was useless, this is a rare tribute. Burra was killed in an air crash in 1937, aged twenty-seven. Many benign interpreters of Forster succeeded him, and when he thought it right to do so Forster also corresponded with them, especially Lionel Trilling and Wilfred H. Stone.

No doubt his habit of looking back over his novels was related to his difficulty in adding to their number. He told T.E. Lawrence that the kind of thing he wanted to write was not for public distribution, citing 'The Life to Come' and implying that tales of homosexual adventure, fulfilment and tragedy were what he felt inspired to write. He needed inspiration; without it there would be no 'real writing'. Lawrence regarded one of these stories, 'Dr Woolacott', written in 1927, as 'the most powerful thing I ever read ... more charged with the real high explosive than anything I've ever met yet'. But inspiration, in the years after *A Passage to India*, seemed to produce only unpublishable 'sexy stories', as he called them, which served only a minority (his favoured word for homosexuals). As early as 1911 he had suffered from 'weariness of the only subject that I both can and may treat – the love of men for women & vice versa'. While *A Passage to India* was still new, he told Siegfried Sassoon he would never write another novel – 'my patience with ordinary people has given out' – though he declared his intention to go on writing. In 1935 he specified his two great, though probably conflicting, ambitions: 'I want to love a young man of the lower classes and be loved by him and even hurt by him. That is my ticket, and then I have wanted to write respectable novels ...' Almost three decades later, in 1964, in his eighty-sixth year, he named economically the force that had kept him from producing more saleable fiction and becoming 'a more famous writer': 'sex'.

Forster loved the East, and especially India. His ethic of tolerance and love ensured his sympathy with subject nations, though he was not uncritical of them, but one cannot reasonably read *A Passage to India* as expressing support for the stronger movement towards Indian independence, which came later. Critics have no trouble finding that it lacks a clear political message, given the absence from the book of the Congress Party and direct allusion to a change of attitude in Anglo-Indians. It had been said that Indians continued to harbour a deep hatred of the British for their conduct during the Mutiny of 1857, and there had been a gross reminder of that event in 1919 at Amritsar, when British Army Indian soldiers had killed many civilians. Yet the only character in Forster's novel close to being an active nationalist is the barrister Hamidullah, whose committee of Hindus, Moslems, Sikhs, Parsis, Jains and Christians 'tried to like one another more than came natural to them' and offered no prospect of liberation. Aziz has no politics at all, only the resentments of the moment and pretty images of a great Islamic past, which Hamidullah thinks just as well, for the young doctor's career might easily be blighted, as we learn from his dealings, early on, with his odious boss, Major Callendar.

The novel makes no direct reference to Amritsar, though Forster was well informed about the massacre, for his friend Malcolm Darling was able to give him a close account of it, having been in the Punjab at the time, but not in Amritsar. The times were bad; India had contributed heavily to the British cause during the First World War, and now soldiers were returning to an economic depression and new laws enforcing colonial rule. Discontent was particularly grave in the Punjab. The Rowlatt Act of 1919 gave the British authorities new powers, and the reaction to these had brought Gandhi, and the Congress Party, to new prominence. There was a popular demand for the release of two leaders of the India Independence movement. When in April 1919 a crowd of unarmed men, women and children gathered in an Amritsar garden near the Golden Temple, many to take part in a Sikh festival, the British general in charge, Reginald Dyer, decided that they constituted a danger to order and made his troops open fire, which they did indiscriminately; the exits were narrow and neither the living nor the wounded could easily escape. Estimates of casualties ran as high as a thousand. Dyer later said not only that his order was justified but that he would have used his machine guns had he been able to bring them to bear. His action was approved and endorsed by his superiors.

At the Amritsar Club, the centre of British social life, his action also met with full approval. Indians had recently assaulted British women, and Darling's account left no doubt that the Club panicked. Darling himself was heavily criticized for having been absent from the city at a time of danger;

he was accused of cowardice and told he should be court-martialled. It is no doubt characteristic of such situations that the colonial power should be confused. The equable Darling, seeing around him 'the old bitterness embittered' – 'the great towns hate us' – was close to believing that Indian independence was 'the only way out of the mess', yet he clearly thought that it would be disastrous. 'Democracy – for India, with her 300 million illiterates – God's truth, we must be possessed. The Gadarene swine are not in it.' Yet if the Indians believed they must have it, 'Let 'em taste the poison they long for.' Darling was a conscientious and temperate man, but he was obviously under great strain. Here he was speaking the language of the Club.

When he came home on leave he discussed the situation with Forster, and although Forster seems to have written nothing specifically about it, that the events in Amritsar influenced *A Passage to India* is virtually certain. The Club, with its arbitrary and hysterical reactions, was after all not simply a Forsterian caricature but the kind of colonialist clique Darling had observed at first hand. He had done much to prove himself a friend to Indians, and his despair at the massacre is evidence of what seemed the ultimate impossibility of such friendships, like the final parting of Fielding and Aziz.

Forster was not exempt from the confusion. His novel is insistent that in India things are never as they seem, nor are the people. On his first visit to India he remarked jokingly in a letter that it was impossible to punish an Indian because Indians ate so little. British visitors observed that Indians had quite different economic and social priorities; Sidney and Beatrice Webb noted that an Indian found it 'extraordinarily difficult to *sweat*: he prefers to waste away in semi-starvation rather than overwork himself. However low his standard of life, his standard of work is lower.' All this led to domestic and economic muddle, of which Forster offered many instances. Muddle was something he deplored in English life but found amusing in India, especially among favoured princes. Sometimes it was the product of worthy motives (Aziz lacking a collar stud because he has gone out of his way to oblige Fielding, Aziz trying to manage the disastrous Marabar expedition); or it might result from liturgical scrupulousness (as when Godbole's puja causes Fielding to miss the train to Marabar) or from the futile good intentions of the bureaucracy (the bridge party) or from the confusions of the trial, a muddle which the magistrate barely manages to control. 'God is love' is muddled into 'God si love'. The British tend to muddle from ignorance, as when Miss Quested raises with Aziz the question of Islamic polygamy. Mrs Moore loses her bearings in a muddle that is almost metaphysical, involving a sudden contempt for marriage and 'personal relations' in general. Nothing is clear; everyone suffers in the confusion, including the white folk; nothing makes sense in their terms and they have no real trust in the place or in its native population. Edward Said remarks that 'the novel's helplessness neither goes all the way and condemns (or defends) British colonialism, nor condemns or defends Indian nationalism'. He is compelled to conclude that the book 'founders on the undodgeable facts of Indian nationalism'. One sees why he reached this conclusion, but it is wrong all the same, failing to understand how it can be that, caught in this dilemma, the book still does not founder, is difficult in some of the ways India is difficult, and, like India, can on occasion be menacingly foreign as well as strange and beautiful.

As I have mentioned, Forster interrupted work on *A Passage to India* in 1913 to compose *Maurice*, and he did not resume until 1922, after his second Indian visit. In between, he did his war service in Alexandria, where he wrote about that city, formed a relationship with a tram-conductor and made the acquaintance of the poet Constantine Cavafy. Once he was back in England at the end of 1919, many preoccupations kept him from the manuscript. But then, again in India, at Dewas in 1921–2, he witnessed, among other things, the Gokul Ashtami festival that gave him the material for the third section of the novel, and with great difficulty he finished it in January 1924. It was published in June of that year.

Forster was now forty-five, and not surprisingly, this latest work gave him further cause to reflect on his creativity. Its success was encouraging, but in early middle age he could not easily accept it as the last demonstration of his creative power. The artist, he said, 'must live his life' – meaning that he must live according to the requirements imposed on him by being an artist; and art was 'the one orderly product' to set against muddle. He told the Northern Irish novelist Forrest Reid, to whom he often confessed his problems, that he worried that when the book seemed to be going well: 'there rises before me my special nightmare – that of the writer as craftsman, natty and deft'. When Reid asked him how his work was getting on, he replied that he was 'dried up. Not in my emotions, but in their expression. I cannot write at all ... The only book I have in my head [*Arctic Summer*] is too like *Howards End* to interest me.' Still, 'To have done good work is something and I don't the least doubt that I have done some.' Years later, while struggling with the Indian novel, he spoke to Lowes Dickinson of his 'creative impotence' and told Siegfried Sassoon that although he was feeling 'no decline in his powers' he feared he would never write another novel after this one; he seemed more interested in 'The Life to Come', one of the risqué stories he had been writing with creative pleasure and felt he must give up; he destroyed several such stories in 1922, but did so sadly. 'Why can't I always be writing things like this?'

While still needing to work on *A Passage to India*, he grumbled about 'the conventionalities of fiction-form' and 'the studied ignorance of novelists'. 'They must recapture their interest in death, not that they ever had it much, but the Middle Ages had it, and the time for re-examination is overdue.' His Alexandrian friend Mohammed was dying yet 'I don't give a damn so far'. He wondered whether the death of his mother would 'shatter' him. 'All this needs mopping up by the novelists.' By 1930, when *A Passage to India* had enjoyed much success, he told his French friend and translator Charles Mauron that he still could not create and complained that he passed a great deal of time 'with people who are (vaguely speaking) my inferiors, and to whom I can very easily be kind'. The mood persisted. In 1943, in a letter to his close friend William Plomer, he lamented the passing of the civilization of Bloomsbury, which nothing had replaced; meanwhile he wasted time 'with second rate people to whom I haven't even any obligation to be kind'. He could not write about ordinary people; he said, more explicitly, that the kind of relationship novelists were supposed to deal with – men and women and love – were no longer of interest to him.

Back in 1913 he had met a fakir at Benares. 'He did *not* sit on spikes and was very charming. We had a long talk chiefly about "inspiration" – i.e. the mental process through which one goes during the act of writing ... I was interested to find that it was the same in his case as mine, though I produce novels and he Sanscrit Poems.' Elsewhere he noted that the fakir explained the Tree of the Universe to him and confirmed that they had had similar experiences when they entered a creative state.

Somehow inspiration offered itself at last, and he finished *A Passage to India*. In 1937, when he looked it over, as his habit was, and felt content, he nonetheless told Christopher Isherwood: 'when writing it I thought it a failure, and it was only owing to Leonard Woolf that I was encouraged to finish it.' Inspiration may have come, as he said it must, from sleep, but it came also from the solicitous and intelligent Woolf, well practised in the vagaries of inspiration. Indeed, Virginia Woolf's was closer to the fakir's experience when Sanskrit poems presented themselves to him. She was about forty-four and her mother had been dead for thirty years when 'one day walking round Tavistock Square I made up, as I sometimes made up my books, *To the Lighthouse* in a great, apparently involuntary rush. My lips seemed syllabling of their own accord as I walked. . . . I wrote the book very quickly; and when it was written I ceased to be obsessed by my mother. I no longer hear her voice; I do not see her. Certainly there she was, in the very centre . . . there she was from the very first.' Woolf did not connect this absence with the unexpected presence of Mrs Dalloway at the end of that novel ('For there she was') but tentatively offered a psychological explanation: that to express the emotion her inspiration offered involved the fading of the vision she had formerly lived with. Whatever one thinks of this explanation – her biographer, Hermione Lee, is sceptical – it is certain that the mother who had been there, in the centre, no longer was. Those lips 'syllabling of their own accord' have an authentic quality; here inspiration is akin to possession.

So, in a sense, is Forster's, though less spectacularly. One could think of the Maharajah, of Bapu Sahib, as having powers not unlike the fakir's, or Godbole's, or Virginia Woolf's. I have mentioned Forster's theory that creative power is independent of intelligence. This may be frivolous but it does allow for inspiration as possession, as the product of dreams rather than intellect. So one might account for the fakir and for the Maharajah, whose chaotic personal life, indicating a catastrophic intellectual disorder, failed to damage the spiritual power to which Forster had access.

Forster had friends deeply affected by Indian religion – Edward Carpenter, for instance and, in a later generation, Isherwood and other Californian exiles like Gerald Heard – but they were students of religious texts, whereas Forster's interest derived largely from a particular person, an eccentric saint.

Forster's orientalism may seem unrelated to his reputation as evangel of a more secular spirituality – the cult of love and 'the beloved republic' – but in the end they probably connect, in the right Forsterian way. Fortunately in the critical year of 1938 he wrote his credo; it is one of his best known essays, called simply 'What I Believe'.

The familiar humorous mild tone of this essay is meant to accommodate the boldness of the claims made by its argument to the unassertive personality of its author. It is a lay sermon and the preacher will make ethical recommendations, but genially and without conceit. He will not stray far beyond the boundaries of what a decent audience will be ready to understand and accept. Times having changed, he will cite not familiar biblical texts but great works or touchstone passages, assuming in his audience a decent or sufficient acquaintance with them, such as the preachers of an earlier generation might have expected of their Bible-reading grandparents. 'What I Believe' has allusions to Shakespeare, Dante, Wagner, Homer, Sophocles, Horace, Keats and Jacopone da Todi, and very likely more. Sometimes he explains them (Fafnir, Brünnhilde, lots more Wagner, Brutus and Cassius in Dante's hell) and sometimes he doesn't. By these means he gently tests our qualifications for membership of the group he will call his aristocracy. How are we to understand the reference to Horace ('like Horace, I see no evidence that each batch of births is superior to the last' – *vixere fortes ante Agamemnona*)? Why is the expression 'change of heart' enclosed in quotation marks? Who made that moving remark about the holiness of the heart's affections? He was certainly one of the chosen, and your recognizing the unexplained allusion to him hints that you may be, too. Who said that the action of beauty was no stronger than a flower? The author has this quotation running in his head, for he uses it again, and again without attribution, in his essay on 'Anonymity'. Do you know where he found it? This is a fairly simple test.

The Italian of the thirteenth-century Spiritual Franciscan poet Jacopone da Todi is a more difficult matter, something for most Anglophone readers to look up. The words quoted by Forster come from one of a series of poems written, with great force and exaltation, in archaic Italian, and called *Laudes*. The poems are addressed to divine Love; the nearest English equivalent, not all that close, might be the baroque religious verse of Richard Crashaw four centuries later. Matthew Arnold knew about Jacopone (see his sonnet 'Austerity of Poetry') and Forster knew his Matthew Arnold; but it happens that in 1919 Evelyn Underhill, author of *Mysticism*, which became the standard English work on the subject, published a biography of Jacopone that made him more accessible and included translations. Underhill was a disciple of Baron von Hügel, who, as Yeats remarked, accepted the miracles of the saints and honoured sanctity. This complicated man – a 'modernist' Roman Catholic – was a theological celebrity in the London of Forster's time and had important friends (A.J. Balfour, for instance), as did Underhill. Forster almost certainly knew Underhill's books, and it seems he was struck by this fragment of Jacopone's verse, which he quotes again, slightly varying the translation, in the essay 'Art for Art's Sake', five years later. It is printed in the same section of *Two Cheers for Democracy*. *Ordina questo amore, O tu che m'ami* – 'O thou who lovest me, set my love in order.'

The interest of the Italian verse lies, for us, in the contexts of its use by Forster. In 'What I Believe' it comes in while he is discussing the need for change 'in the sphere of morals and politics' – he says Jacopone was expressing the same desire in his poems. An antithesis between order and 'muddle' is a recurring element in Forster's thought, and he sees that Jacopone knew it existed and sought by prayer to eliminate muddle. But Forster is sure the desired change will not come about even if 'the Saviour of the Future' should arrive, collect Forster's band of aristocrats, and set to work. The second use of the verse occurs in a passage lamenting the apparent lack of order in the heavens since the intrusion of Einstein. That lack is said to leave us with only two possibilities of order, the first of which emanates from 'the divine author, the mystic harmony'. For this we have only the evidence of 'adepts', which cannot be lightly dismissed; but he declines to consider it, and instead passes to the only remaining possibility of order, which is art, 'the one orderly product which our muddling race has produced'. Again the antithesis order/muddle, here firmly related to the praise and the defence of art.

This idea of order is a central tenet of Forster's faith. It is an aesthetic imperative to which he is always faithful when serious, as he is here. Art – if you like, he will say 'art for art's sake' – is, as Baudelaire put it, *le meilleur témoignage que nous puissions donner de notre dignité*. It is the best evidence we could give of our dignity, and it is a mystery of such importance that it must by all means be defended; in speaking of it one must, if necessary, protect it with language borrowed from religion, from the language of Jacopone's prayers, because the little secular florilegium of poems provided may not be strong enough – no stronger than a flower, no better equipped to withstand the destructive forces of an opponent named 'rage' but also known as mortality and time.

How surprising it is that in 'What I Believe', just as he is reflecting on order, and on Jacopone's words, Forster (not a writer prone to unconsidered expressions on serious occasions) should say that 'the indwelling spirit will have to be restated if it is to calm the waters again'! The 'indwelling spirit' is an expression with a long pulpit history; as it happens it was used by Forster's kinsman Robert Isaac Wilberforce in his book *Incarnation*, as the *OED* attests ('an immediate indwelling of the Godhead in the whole body of mankind'). This Wilberforce, one of the three sons of the great William, seems to have been a theologian of some repute, an associate of Newman and Manning, and a convert to Rome; perhaps it was only in comparison with the galaxy of talent to be found in the Clapham Sect and more generally in the tradition of Forster's family that he could be described as tedious. According to sharp-tongued Aunt Marianne herself, he was known in the family as 'dull Robert', and he makes what she would very likely have called a deservedly brief appearance in Forster's biography, *Marianne Thornton*.

So the 'indwelling spirit' is an expression as old as Wyclif and still redolent of studious Victorian vicarages. Forster, though tempted by the thought of a secular equivalent, reminds himself that he is not a Christian and almost at once withdraws the idea, apologizing for even the trace of 'faith' it introduces. He says that spirit will have to be 'restated'. But how? He does not know. He has come to understand that tolerance, good temper and sympathy are no longer enough: their action is no stronger than a flower – the quotation perhaps serving as a test – if you don't recognize it you may not be eligible for admission to the post-Apostolic interplanetary coterie to be defined later in the piece. But the readers he must have envisaged for this essay might be expected to feel easy with and informed by such casual allusions. That is why they belong to the coterie, the right kind of clique. 'The people I admire most are those who are sensitive and want to create something or discover something ... They found religions, great or small, or they produce literature and art, or they do disinterested scientific research' or, as an alternative of last resort, bring up their children creatively. And then, of course, they die, as indeed everybody does, elect or not. And that fact is here produced in contempt of dictators and in support of Jacopone: 'the memory of birth and the expectation of death always lurk within the human being' and these termini are the property of every individual. Not for the first nor the last time we hear that note: death is necessary to full human expression, to what Forster in that highly idiomatic passage from *The Longest Journey* which I quoted in my third chapter calls 'greatness'.

'What I Believe' is indeed a secular and literary lay sermon, but the religious undertones – their registration and their rejection – are necessary to its success. Forster is aware of what he is doing, introducing the problem of religion at the earliest possible moment, when he says that he does not believe in belief, that his motto is 'Lord, I disbelieve – help thou my unbelief'. In the biblical original 'help' has the sense of 'cure' rather than 'assist' (as in Shakespeare's 'Who is Sylvia?', where 'Love doth to her eyes repair/To help him of his blindness'). But Forster, of course, isn't seeking a cure for unbelief. He already knows what such a cure must be: 'personal relationships', a panacea he had known of since he was a Cambridge undergraduate, though a worry about the destructive power of modern psychology can shake his belief in the very idea of a person and so of personal relationships. Nevertheless, personal relationships are all we have, apart, of course, from death. He develops the idea, emphasizing the need for trust, even when it is liable to be betrayed.

Despite the seriousness of the topic the essay has a prevailing tone of clerical humour, the sort that can be attributed to professional geniality while at the same time suggesting that it must not for that reason be disregarded. Hence the impressive but unassertive (and unacknowledged) allusion – all competent readers will recognize it without difficulty – to the first chapter of St John's Gospel. It is revealed that one's own 'little light' is 'not the only one which the darkness does not comprehend.' 'Comprehend' used to mean 'encompass', 'grasp', 'lay hold of', senses which live virtually in this Johannine context alone, or in allusions to it. The trembling flames by means of which the Forsterian aristocrats make it known that they have not succumbed to cultural darkness have been lit at John 1:4. They are visible but 'ironic', in Auden's 'September 1, 1939', where the genial company envisaged by Forster has, rather grimly, become 'the Just': 'Ironic points of light/ Flash out wherever the Just/ Exchange their messages:/ May I, composed like them/ Of Eros and of dust,/ Beleaguered by the same/ Negation and Despair,/ Show an affirming flame.' This poem, which Auden came to detest, also contains the line 'We must love one another or die'. As the poet later rather pedantically pointed out, we are here offered a false alternative, for loving one another won't stop us from dying; but Forster read it as a slogan so inspiring that he expressed a willingness to follow Auden anywhere.

The famous undertaking to betray his country rather than betray his friend follows. Its true sense lies not in the parallels with Brutus and Cassius, but in the more plausible assertion that a requirement to suffer may lie at the back of every creed, even the creed of personal relationships, a point made in the essay: 'probably one won't have to make the "agonizing choice" between betraying a friend or betraying one's country'; 'still, there lies at the back of every creed something terrible and hard for which the worshipper may one day be required to suffer ...'

Having explained Democracy and its limits, Forster touches on his utopia, the Swinburnian 'Love, the beloved Republic, which feeds upon Freedom and lives'. The inhabitants or claimants to citizenship of that state are, as we have seen, very various: they consist of those who care nothing for power, who found religions, produce literature and art, or are just privately creative, which they may prove by bringing up their children decently. Creativity is opposed to success; 'the progress of creation', independent of success, is itself an achievement.

The ideal citizens of a Forsterian republic would not easily be recognized as democrats, for they form a kind of aristocracy – not an aristocracy of power or influence but 'of the sensitive, the considerate and the plucky'. Its members are of all nations and classes; when they meet there is a secret understanding between them. Some may be ascetics; let them be, though the writer doesn't really approve, so long as they are still sensitive, considerate and plucky. 'Their temple, as one of them remarked, is the Holiness of the Heart's Affection' – and presumably they will all know where that allusion comes from. They are Forster's Aristocracy, knowable only to one another, secret lovers, their signal lights flickering yet uncomprehended (in the archaic sense at least) in a darkening world.

'What I Believe' is Forster's best-known essay, a credo of obvious appeal, and the above discussion of it may well be regarded as far from satisfactory as an explanation of the warm regard in which it continues to be held. The problem is that the whole thing is both too easy and too taxing, loveable now, sharp later. Christianity, the model explicitly disallowed, is smuggled back in, leaving one to wonder whether its presence was intentional or accidental. And somebody should

write a study of the rhetoric of whimsy, its possibilities for
irony, its tendency to give points away as well as scoring them.

Another, tamer, term for the philosophy or politic outlined
in 'What I Believe', and one that Forster would have accepted,
is 'liberal'. He liked the old liberal values and amenities and
thought the contemporary novel all the poorer in that it had
given up the old liberal subjects.

> So marriage, love, friendship, family feuds, social nuances,
> lawsuits about property, illegitimate children, failures on the
> stock exchange – all the products of liberalism in fact, all
> essentially the subject matter of Dickens, Trollope, Jane
> Austen, Arnold Bennett – don't serve the modern novelist so
> well. He doesn't even find death very useful. Death, as an
> extinguisher of consciousness, has its importance, but since
> the characters are not presented as entities, as inexplicable
> individuals, the disappearance of one of them can't be expected
> to upset the reader . . .

So death is another liberal benefit we have sacrificed. This
new world, the world of the modern novel that must manage
without death, is not the world of *Ulysses* nor yet the world
of *The Waves*. It has tried to replace that old liberal world of
sturdy constructions in solid mahogany, a world in which the
characters bear the marks of mortality and are willing to die
in the more or less usual way, as many of Forster's own
characters notoriously do.

But in fact his novels aren't really like those old liberal
products; as he insists when defending himself against Virginia
Woolf, he has his own method, his own creativity, and it
depends on important incursions from another world that
could not be called 'liberal' or 'solid'. It must be insubstantial,
mythical, and it must coexist with what, after generations of

training in the conventions of realism, all normal persons can be persuaded to regard as reality. Neither of these worlds can be neglected without great loss. The threat, for Forster, was mostly to the supernatural element. The stories he most enjoyed writing tended to be too heavy with the supernatural to please most readers. Rather strangely, he reproached Henry James for lacking it. One of the things he liked about D.H. Lawrence was a certain glamorous *Aberglaube*.

Although Forster decided he could not accept him into full intimacy, he never lost his admiration for Lawrence, and he did presumably think of him as the kind of creator who had his approval in 'What I Believe'. It may surprise a modern reader that he particularly admired *The Plumed Serpent*, a religious myth or fantasy that dealt in its way, not at all obviously Forster's way, with personal relationships, while regarding *Women in Love* as disappointing. Despite the array of differences that decisively separated them, each of these novelists had some understanding of the importance of the other, though they blundered when trying to express their opinions. And well they might, for both, in their quite different ways, were bullies, and they perhaps could not solve their social problems. For example, Lawrence had experienced but failed to enjoy the company at King's, as one might have expected; in his opinion, they over-simplified other people there, a view Forster came close to agreeing with.

During a weekend spent together Forster and Lawrence contrived, without forfeiting mutual respect, to feel how great the distance was between them. Lawrence thought he could see Forster 'dodging himself' and found the sight pitiful. His immediate remedy for Forster's apparent ills was that he should take a woman – a therapy Forster had never yet contemplated and was very unlikely to. So they corresponded and respected one another, and after Lawrence died Forster wrote that he regarded him as 'one of the glories of our twentieth-century literature', and 'the greatest imaginative novelist of his generation'. On the same occasion T.S. Eliot wrote disputing that judgement: 'unless we know exactly what Mr Forster means by *greatest*, *imaginative*, and *novelist* I submit that this judgment is meaningless'. Forster replied, 'Mr Eliot duly entangles me in his web. He asks what exactly I mean by "greatest", "imaginative" and "novelist" and I cannot say. Worse still, I cannot even say what "exactly" means – only that there are occasions when I would rather be a fly than a spider, and the death of D.H. Lawrence is one of these.' Here, if anywhere, is an occasion for Forster's audience to stand and applaud.

Lawrence was not cut out to be considerate, and Forster was unlikely ever to be a serious candidate for his utopia, Rananim, where there would be no class and no money – a real community, dedicated to the idea of 'many fulfilled individualities seeking greater fulfilment'. Forster had no comparable utopia, only the signal lights of the uncomprehended; his idea was more abstract, and probably entirely male. When Frieda Lawrence added a friendly postscript to a letter of her husband's, Forster let them know he refused to 'have dealings with a firm'. It may be asked whether this gesture qualified as 'considerate'. No doubt Frieda could take it. Lawrence was 'cross' and wrote to tell Forster that there were 'some things you should not write in your letters', perhaps remembering the dignified reproof addressed by Mrs Wilcox to Margaret Schlegel in *Howards End* ('You should not have written me such a letter').

He might sometimes have agreed with Lawrence that the ruin of Europe was caused by the failure of women to understand their true role, which was not the quest for sexual satisfaction but submission to the male. That would be a very strong version of Forster's distaste for all but a few privileged women. 'As usual,' he writes in a letter, 'the women have precipitated the trouble and make no attempt to understand each other.' When he met Christabel Pankhurst he found her 'very able, very clever and very unpleasant.' Although she 'talked a certain amount of rot' he 'agreed with most of her remarks' but he showed no continuing interest. In some respects a very close friend of Virginia Woolf's, he could appraise her with deliberate coolness after her death, remarking that her feminism reinforced her detachment from the working classes. (So far as I know there is no record of his response to her being in 1918, along with other women over thirty, at last allowed to have a vote in parliamentary elections.) He disliked the idea that he and she were inevitably competitive. In 1915 he wrote a comfortable note to himself, saying that her work was 'certainly inferior to mine', though 'more adventurous'. As more of her books appeared he became more generous, reviewing *To the Lighthouse* very favourably and greatly admiring *The Waves*; reading it, he said, made one feel one was dealing with a classic. He saw her as altering the novel in a way he felt he must admire, though he did not greatly like it. She in her turn could be severe on his work. He was irritatingly evasive: 'We want to make Mr Forster stand and deliver.' He was cross at this and disputed her adverse comments: 'I don't believe my method's wrong.' When he wrote comments on some promising writers – Woolf, Walter de la Mare, Katherine Mansfield, Norman Douglas – Woolf's *Night and Day* seems to have struck him as the best any of them had done, but he still thought it unlikely that any of them would revive the waning vitality of the English novel, arguing that they were altogether too '*modern*' in method. It may be said that with the notable exception of Proust, and despite his favouring experiment in principle, he tended to retreat when confronted with big or adventurous modern novelists.

In general Woolf found him 'an unworldly, transparent character, whimsical and detached, caring very little I should think what people say, & with a clear idea of what he wishes ... he resembles a vaguely rambling butterfly and there is no intensity or rapidity about him'. She did not like his blend of realism and soul or spirit, and by saying so hurt Forster more than she had wanted. As for him, as we saw, he 'waited for her to snap'. It sounds like a tense friendship. But she valued his praise more than anybody's, and he came to see high merit in her later fictional experiments. One might have thought him a perfect reader for *Between the Acts*, but I find no mention of it, even in the memorial lecture he gave in Cambridge in 1941, which touches on most of her books. But he praised her imaginative power, a quality he profoundly admired, while conscious that his own was fitful.

Forster was justified in speaking of his 'method', for he had one. Broadly speaking, he developed it in order to accommodate in his fiction a union between the solid and the mythical, or perhaps one should say 'the magical', or whatever adjective seems best suited to the presence in his work of that quality of the religious or supernatural that he found lacking in James. As I've said, he did not share the theoretical positions of Percy Lubbock and Henry James and, in particular, he was sceptical about their doctrine of the fixed point of view, arguing that if an author could establish a point of view in one particular character he could as well do so with all of them. Hence his long guerrilla action against James, though he recognized a great talent and a great man. Although he would not say so to Lubbock, a friend and once his boss, he privately did not think much of *The Craft of Fiction*, though he praised it in *Aspects*.

His method was quite different; it was Wagnerian – he had known *The Ring* since his early twenties, when he pursued it around Europe – and, better still, it was Proustian. So, it might be said, were most members of the Bloomsbury coterie, but they did not see, as he did, how the Proustian interest could suggest new technical resources, so that without any need to abandon older ideas about characters he could enable the narrative to acquire secret senses, at the expense of gaining weight, a Proustian feature reflected in other modern masterpieces but not imitated by Forster, whose novels are all of the fashionable Jane Austenish length that went best with a retail price of about 6/-.

As I've mentioned, the important reason he gave for his long abstention from fiction was just that he couldn't interest himself in the love of man for woman and vice versa. It was peculiarly his problem, and the examples of Edward Carpenter and of D.H. Lawrence could not make it go away. Lawrence constructed a mythical religion – the 'indwelling spirit' is perhaps love and creativity under another name; certainly a quiet, ecumenical formula compared with Lawrence's Quetzalcoatl, yet still qualifying as a touch of the supernatural. Forster's unpublished novel *Maurice* has a happy ending; he felt this to be a necessary compensation for the difficulties, in his day, of homosexual partnerships. He also wrote a good many stories, some of which he destroyed, in which gay relationships, sometimes happy, occur. His interest in fantasy called for a whole chapter in *Aspects of the Novel* and it affected some of the stories, including those collected posthumously in *The Life to Come*. He thought this was the kind of thing he did well, and wished he could go on doing them. Oliver Stallybrass, who edited these tales, wonders discreetly whether Lawrence's fascination with 'Dr Woolacott' doesn't say more 'about his powerfully developed death-wish' than about the quality of the story. It seems likely that most modern readers would incline to the editor's view.

*

Lawrence had been under the impression that Forster was interested in Buddhism. His early mentor G.L. Dickinson may have encouraged such an interest, but he was not, like Dickinson, a professional student of religions or, like Edward Carpenter, a dedicated amateur. As a member of the Society of Psychical Research Dickinson accepted the Society's rule that certain 'paranormal' phenomena called for sceptical examination excluding commitment to a particular orthodoxy. Forster seems to have been sceptical of this scepticism. Psychical research, an important concern of many powerful intellects at the time, he described in his biography of Dickinson as the 'dustbin of the spirit'. Buddhism was perhaps a more serious matter, associated not with European mediums and seances but with the East, an area always fascinating to Forster. Yet his interest in the subject seems to be largely aesthetic – more or less a matter of caves and monuments. As he himself noticed, Buddhism was virtually extinct in modern India. On the other hand the two predominant Indian religions, Islam and Hinduism, were in different ways of serious concern to him; both were central to his idea of the East, and to his understanding of the ways in which they retained their power just as the power of European religions seemed to be fading. In a letter written in September 1921 he says, 'I do like Islam, though I have had to come through Hinduism to discover it.' And he contrasts the 'mess and profusion and confusion' of the Gokul Ashtami celebrations (which, we learn elsewhere, he regarded as among the most important experiences of his entire life) with the feeling of standing on a mountain and listening to the distant call of the muezzin. He evidently shared Aziz's pleasure when he discovered that Mrs Moore, contrary to expectation, removed her shoes to enter a mosque, as he did himself when, as sometimes happened, he went into a mosque to meditate. With his love of order, especially intellectual order, he preferred Islamic intellect and order to the happiness of the messy improvised rituals of the Gokul Ashtami celebrations and the hilarious profundities of the nativity of Krishna, wonderful though they were.

The contemporary intellectual reaction against Christianity was accompanied by a new curiosity about other religions, old and new; and sometimes serious men and women mixed all that was new and old into doctrines now blended for the first time. Suffragettes might embrace a faith as remote from their political programme as theosophy. Fabians, whose society was originally called the Fellowship of the New Life, had what Samuel Hynes describes as a 'patchwork membership' – groups advocating Marxism, neo-Malthusianism, Christianity, atheism – until it moved, gradually as was only proper, towards the establishment of unity of political purpose as an instrument of socialist propaganda. Hynes lists many organizations flourishing in the late years of the nineteenth century which apparently had little in common save a desire to reform society or perhaps, more largely, the world: the Democratic Federation, the Hermetic Order of the Golden Dawn, the National Anti-Vaccination League, the Society for Psychical Research, and the Theosophical Society. All were opposed to conventional Victorian moral and social ideals, and all contributed to a 'restlessness' that persisted, as Hynes says, throughout the Edwardian period. It was noted by authority, which is always suspicious of restlessness; and thus began a struggle to control the activities of anarchists, and also to censor the reports of sexologists and the imaginations of novelists and playwrights. There could be no easy agreement between those who by one means or another sought a New Life, a plan that would require huge alterations to the nation's institutions, and to the politicians and judges who thought such ideas self-evidently destructive of the family and society, its laws, its schools, its morale in general.

If all the unorthodox notions of the period could be summed up in one man, that man was Edward Carpenter. Forster came to know him well, and he may now be best remembered from Forster's account of a memorable visit he paid to the sage in 1913, at his smallholding in Derbyshire. This was already a place of pilgrimage; Lawrence had visited Carpenter, as Dickinson had before him, taking along Roger Fry, who painted Carpenter's portrait. Doubtless both Fry and Dickinson discussed Carpenter with Forster, who would have read at least Carpenter's most celebrated book, the Whitmanesque *Towards Democracy*, and was probably familiar with some of his many other works. Unlike the one he made to the Lawrences, Forster's visit to Carpenter was a complete success. George Merrill, Carpenter's housemate or companion, touched Forster on his backside – 'gently and just above the buttocks' – and this touch 'seemed to go straight through the small of my back into my ideas, without involving my thoughts'. (Love, as Forster learned from his friend the Maharajah of Chhatarpur, a devotee of Krishna, was the only power that could keep thought out.) The result was the novel *Maurice*, written with unaccustomed speed though frequently revised.

Carpenter was well known as a champion of many ideas and activities opposed, though quite calmly, to conventional opinion. Sheila Rowbotham's excellent biography reminds us that he absorbed and explained and synthesized practically every advanced idea of the time. He was a rebel to his upper-class family – socialist and sometimes anarchist, utopian, vegetarian, pianist, advocate of 'free and equal human relations' and of the 'simple life' (Shaw called him 'the noble savage'), keen homosexual (he wrote a book on what he called 'homo-genity', refusing to use the term 'homosexual' because it is the product of an illicit union between a Latin and a Greek word) and all-round seeker after the New Life.

Carpenter gave up a Cambridge fellowship to live first in Sheffield, later on a rural Derbyshire property. He liked to have sex with working-class men, and somehow managed to do so without getting into trouble. He was highly esteemed for this as well as other distinctive beliefs and activities; it became the custom for curious intellectuals to visit him, inter-ested not only in his political and social opinions but also in the mysticism that accompanied and blended with them. His very unusual manner of life ensured a large measure of fame or notoriety, and he became famous as the gentleman who defiantly pioneered the wearing of sandals, which he made according to a Kashmiri design, sometimes measuring his visitors' feet for the purpose. Just as Shaw and some other Fabians accepted the teaching of Dr Gustav Jaeger and wore woollen garments because good health depended on the dis-posal of bodily poisons through the skin – a process frustrated by the wearing of linen or cotton – so Carpenter regarded shoes, like other features of upper-class dress, as impeding the freedom of the body, in this instance the feet, though the freedom of the sexual organs was of comparable concern. He fought for local as well as national causes, defending, for example, the rights of local young men to bathe naked. He could on occasion be politically active in London and took part in the great but useless demonstration of Sunday, 13 November 1887, when the united forces of the Left took on the police in Trafalgar Square and were crushed. During the debacle he was struck in the face and manhandled by 'that crawling thing, a policeman'.

But he was a gentle man, and violence was not his choice;

moreover, as Rowbotham shows, he was capable of changing the world in other ways. Some of his ideas were so far from being impractical dreams that they were to become familiar features of modern Britain in the forms, for instance, of garden cities and progressive schools and sexual freedom. He was the enemy of everything that contributed to 'the starving of the human heart', and many different sorts of people, including Forster, loved and respected him for that.

The clearest indication of Forster's faith in Carpenter may be found in a letter written from Alexandria in 1916, in which Forster, addressing Carpenter as his 'greatest comfort', vividly describes his unsatisfied sexual craving: 'I know that though you have heard this and sadder cases 1000 times before, you will yet be sympathetic ...' Dickinson's interest in Carpenter was bound to stimulate Forster.

Carpenter himself – a man who, it was said, had slept with Walt Whitman and was certainly a favoured correspondent of that great man – had a strong romantic appeal. Forster's views on sex were much like Carpenter's – both wanted sex with working-class men, and Forster would have liked a permanent gay relationship like the one Carpenter enjoyed with Merrill. Short of that he could enjoy comradeship, a Carpenterian condition that could be enjoyed in a form better suited to his style of life. Carpenter came from the same moneyed class as Forster himself, experienced in his education the same oppression, the same snobbery and eventually the same freedom; and like him, he deplored the undeveloped heart. Carpenter had been much affected by India and was a student of Hindu scripture; so both men were devoted to India and the 'East' more generally. They both loved music and played the piano. Both bore 'the tattoo-marks of gentility', as Rowbotham puts it, and both, despite much effort, found difficulty in cross-class relations unless they had a sexual basis and sometimes a financial aspect also.

There were possibilities of comradeship, even of intimacy; but Forster was less bold, and Carpenter's defiant and open break with the habits and conventions of his class was one that he did not make. His first meeting with Carpenter finally came about by the accident that he was, roughly, in the vicinity of the Carpenter ménage because his mother had been ordered to take the waters at Harrogate and he was in dutiful attendance, making sure that she did so, a characteristic and recurrent dilemma, though Forster had more freedom of movement – in London, in Alexandria, in India – than might have been expected from such a relationship. He quite often, and quite rightly, presented himself as a man caught between two epochs, one comfortable and constricted, desirable though limiting; the other an age whose changed rules fascinated him because, if only things were a little different, he might live in it with one lover or with many, an age freed from the bonds of the vicious (and quite recently enacted) law under which Oscar Wilde had suffered, in which he could be himself and have his working-class lovers with no obligation of secrecy, no fear. Carpenter lived not in accordance with the style of the moment to which chance had consigned him, but as far as possible as he would in a new, more liberated epoch. His book *Love's Coming of Age*, widely read, made him the most prominent challenger of conventional morality. But even he found the old age offered much he was unwilling or unable to leave behind – much that he, like Forster, included in his idea of the liberal tradition (like good furniture, many books, solicitors, good manners).

Though untidy in his dress, Forster was normally what is nowadays called a 'suit'. He adapted himself at appropriate moments to Indian forms of dress but it is difficult to think of him wearing sandals in occidental society. Nor was he interested in the idea of handsome clothes; Carpenter was much more of a swell, and it is in that role that he appears in Roger

Fry's portrait. Elegance was not an aim of Forster's, except in the matter of prose style, which remained of importance whatever the cultural circumstances.

When Carpenter died Forster wrote as follows: 'Astonishing how he drains away ... I suppose there was something there, but as soon as one touches it it's gone. Slow but steady decline of power.' It was a fate he doubtless feared for himself, but Forster's perception may have been affected by the physical decline of Carpenter before his death in 1929. In one of his Indian broadcasts years later, in 1944 – the centenary of Carpenter's birth – he remembers his friend's humour, his praise of human love and the beauty of the countryside; he admires the activity and achievements of his life despite the wretchedness of his end; and he remembers that he had been a lively, indeed an athletic man, noted for his energy in support of so many admirable causes, but denied the happiness of work and friendship in his last years.

Carpenter, in his thought, in his costume, and in his social and sexual life, represented the New Age. A recent *Observer* headline calls him 'the gay godfather of the British left' – slightly absurd, it must be said, yet correctly indicating an admirable boldness in matters both public and private that must have helped prepare the way for the Wolfenden Report of 1957 and its belated sequel, the liberating Sexual Offences Act of 1967. 'He was a very good man, certainly an unusual one, possibly a great one ... he had many activities: a poet, a prose writer, a prophet, a socialist, a mystic, a manual labourer, an anti-vivisectionist, an art critic, etc.: and he did all these things without being a prig.' He added, in a more critical spirit, that Carpenter had 'no conception of the lives of the poor'. (Forster said of himself that in 1914 [*aet.* 35] he himself had a comparable defect, for he 'was ignorant of class. It stimulated my imagination – that was all.')

Determined to find out about the workers, to purge the new world of snobbery and prejudice, Carpenter had tried to abandon his class, but he remained suspicious of other members of it, of Forster for instance – because, like himself, Forster had the disadvantage of an academic education. He hated industrialism. He believed in love, and in the possibility of making a world in which love would conquer its enemies, snobbery, respectability and poverty. Forster's Indian audience (like Forster himself) would have been be glad to hear that it had been a visit to India that changed Carpenter's life by introducing him to the *Bhagavad-Gita*. 'He was obliged,' says Forster, 'to look outside his own race for wisdom.' And in its way that remark applies also to Forster.

The piece ends with a cool eulogy. At more or less the same time Forster wrote another broadcast (or another version of this memorial) in which he points out mildly that Carpenter's socialism hadn't entailed his giving up a useful private income of £500 a year. Forster had his reasons for approving of that precaution. Carpenter may have espoused all manner of admirably quixotic principles, but he was not a fool. To his credit, Forster adds, he had no racial prejudice. As for his socialism, society at large was far from ready for it when Carpenter was writing his propaganda, and it was farther than ever from it at the time of writing.

All the same, Carpenter was 'a very wonderful man ... he stood closer to the stuff of life than anybody I have met with, with the possible exception of Bapu Sahib', the Maharajah who meant so much to Forster and of whom I shall say more later. Carpenter pretty exactly fits Forster's idea of one kind of creative person. He or she must be making something; it needn't be something of great value or beauty – his writing in both prose and verse was poor, but the point is that the work has involved the person concerned in a disinterested exercise of creative power, an achievement that has nothing to do with success. Such persons, however they apply their talents, by whatever they choose to perform creatively, are nevertheless to be distinguished from persons more fully endowed, who experience 'the creative state'. (In another form this is the difference between creative persons and critics, whom Forster regards as almost useless.)

He explains the true creative state in a lecture he gave at Harvard in 1947.

> In [it] a man is taken out of himself. He lets down as it were a bucket into his subconscious, and draws up something which is normally beyond his reach. He mixes this thing with his normal experiences, and out of the mixture he makes a work of art. [It] is a blend of realism and 'magic'. It may be a good work of art or a bad one ... but whether it is good or bad it will have been compounded in this unusual way, and he will wonder afterwards how he did it. Such seems to be the creative process.

It is interesting that the ability to benefit by this process, which is said to be akin to dreaming, is not a guarantee of quality in the waking result. It may be entitled to be regarded as a work of art and it may not; it may be an orderly product and it may not; but the person who had the dream, who, like Jacopone prayed for order, is nevertheless rather special. 'The artist will tend to be an outsider in the society to which he has been born, and ... the nineteenth century conception of him as a Bohemian was not inaccurate', though it needed some qualifications: it wrongly assumed that there could be an economic system where art could be a full-time job; 'it introduced the fallacy that only art matters; and it over-stressed idiosyncrasy and waywardness'. Better this excess than capitulation to enemies of art and order. Artists, presumably the bad ones as well as the good, can reasonably demand state support, even while it is admitted that the state doesn't understand what they are doing; it is the duty of the state and its agents to give him his way, for if they interfere with his experiments and give too much weight to his inability to fit in (and it is true that he will very likely be touched by the vatic madness Plato describes in the *Phaedrus*) they will be reducing order, and 'the development of human sensitiveness in directions away from the average citizen'.

The creative artist is obviously not one to obey orders; his discipline is self-imposed and likely to be aesthetic rather than social or moral. 'He may wish to practise art for art's sake'; the expression is not ridiculous because it indicates the truth that 'art is a self-contained harmony'. 'Art is valuable not because it is educational (though it may be), not because it is recreative (though it may be), not because everyone enjoys it (for everybody does not), not even because it has to do with beauty. It is valuable because it has to do with order, and creates little worlds of its own, possessing internal harmony, in the bosom of this disordered planet.' What enables it to do so is a capacity that may sometimes cause disorder and misunderstanding in that planet, but it is still responsible for the order of art's little worlds.

As an artist who understands and can illustrate creative order Forster chooses Paul Claudel. Asked about inspiration Claudel replies: 'I do not speak what I wish, but I conceive in sleep. And I cannot explain whence I draw my breath, for it is my breath that is drawn out of me. ... I open my mouth, I breathe in the air, I breathe it out. I restore it in the form of an intelligible word.'

Claudel links inspiration with life, and expiration with

death, which, as we have seen before, is a vital preoccupation of Forster's. Forster, I think, was not quite as pretentious as Claudel, but he was clearly familiar with the experience of inspiration. It could happen in quite humble circumstances, when it might be brought on by the mere sight of a pen. It might produce very ordinary pieces of writing, mere criticism, or it might carry with it promises, often disappointed, of achievement, of art. Forster offers an instance from his own experience. A story called 'The Rock' came to him on what seemed a swarming inspiration but it was no good, no editor would touch it: 'My inspiration had been genuine but worthless, like so much inspiration ...' Thanks to the assiduity of a later editor one can read 'The Rock' in the Abinger edition of *The Life to Come*. Even worthless products of inspiration can be saved from the oblivion to which earlier editors had condemned them.

An important group of essays, collected in Part II of *Two Cheers for Democracy*, mostly written in the early days of the Second World War, reflected a concern, widely shared in those years, about the future of the arts and the prospects for order and culture – indeed for what Forster would call 'civilization' – in a future which few, at the time, could think of as likely to be happy or orderly. As he saw them, the prospects looked better for working-class people (there will be work and play for them, though 'the work will be mechanical and the play frivolous'). But there were other citizens to be considered. Almost as important as artists, and indeed often filling the same role, was the rather small population of 'cultivated people'. Forster noted hopefully that there seemed to be more of them around since the previous war (would they, one wonders, be those readers of 'What I Believe' who could instantly identify the quotations?) and he cited Virginia

Woolf's biography of Roger Fry as evidence of this improvement; but it remained true that 'we are a drop in the ocean'. 'We' have been entrusted with a tradition that goes back three thousand years (to Homer, one supposes) but a new ruling class wants none of it, its members happy to pass their time arguing about 'the quickest way to get from Balham to Ealing' and, presumably, rarely approaching Bloomsbury. 'I know a few working-class people who enjoy culture,' says Forster in a revealing aside, 'but as a rule I am afraid to bore them with it lest I lose the pleasure of my acquaintance.' But the pleasures of culture are rather like religion – if you enjoy them you want to pass them on. To refrain from doing so is tantamount to forbidding the spread of the Gospel. Of course 'we' don't want to sound like missionaries, but it should surely be possible to persuade likeable and intelligent people that there is pleasure to be had from 'Sophocles, Velasquez, Henry James'.

It is a strategy that sounds unlikely to convince those who enjoy arguing about the best route to Ealing; and as for the heroic autodidacts of Jonathan Rose, they were either converted already or damned, like Leonard Bast with his tell-tale lilting step. In any case one prefers the Maharajah, Forsterian in his willingness to sacrifice his principles rather than his friends, famous for being silly, and capable of supposing that God suffers from intermittent attacks of attention disorder, always returning eventually to his task of care, his role as Friend.

The Second World War compelled Forster into conspicuous public life, notably as chair of the National Council for Civil Liberties, and beyond that he had, and kept, a surprisingly large circle of friends and acquaintances, most of them very fond of him. We learn from Christopher Isherwood's Diary that he arrived in England from California on 22 January 1947 and while staying with John Lehmann 'saw Forster,

[Bob] Buckingham, [Rupert] Doone, [Robert] Medley, [Louis] MacNeice, Peter Viertels, Henry Green, [William] Plomer, Alan Ross, Keith Vaughan, [Joe] Ackerley, [William] Robson-Scott (an old Berlin friend)'. Within the next few days Isherwood saw Benjamin Britten and Peter Pears, stayed with Forster in his London flat at Chiswick, lunched with Brian Howard and supped with the [Cyril] Connollys and with Guy Burgess and his lover. He spent a day with the [Edward] Upwards, and bought a Keith Vaughan painting. After a good deal more of this he sailed to New York in the *Queen Elizabeth*, moved into the apartment of Auden's friends James and Tania Stern and invited Forster, who had arrived earlier by air, to supper. Then he stayed with Auden, later visiting him on Fire Island before sailing to South America. We next find him with Truman Capote, meeting Lincoln Kirstein, having a reunion with Stephen Spender, having drinks with John Gielgud, and so on.

It seemed worth making this random list of cultivated people whose numbers were said to be growing, and perhaps asking what it says about the company Forster kept in the space of a week or two. Some of the names are of people within what might be called his inner circle: Bob Buckingham, his police-man friend, William Plomer, poet and novelist, Joe Ackerley, literary editor of *The Listener*, famous for loving his dog, Tulip. Another member of this circle was Sebastian Sprott, who later got rid of 'Sebastian' and became 'Jack', once a Fellow of King's and an Apostle, a lover of J.M. Keynes and a protégé of Lady Ottoline Morell; later a professor of Philosophy, then of Psychology, at Nottingham University and the friend chosen by Forster as his literary executor; but he died within a year of Forster and his duties passed to King's. He arrived in Forster's circle via Ackerley's gay London group. All were important persons in Forster's later life. Doone, a dancer originally, and Medley, a painter, were a couple from the world of theatre and ballet. As we have seen Britten and Pears became close friends of Forster. Guy Burgess was the Cambridge spy everybody knew.

Every name listed here belongs, presumably, to a member of that cultivated minority of which Forster spoke, and they look like a sparkling company. Nor should one suppose he inhabited only its margins. One might have expected him to be more interested than he showed himself to be in Upward, an early Cambridge friend of Isherwood, with whom he was co-author of the surrealist Mortmere stories; later, he was the author of a dialectically planned and autobiographical trilogy, *The Spiral Ascent*, a work still honoured by some on the left. He died recently, aged 105, having continued to produce his sometimes eerie short stories almost to the end.

Upward is one of those writers who meet Forster's requirement for creativity at a high level. Henry Green, a great virtuoso of the novel, another inspired creator, gets a mention but otherwise no show of interest. Forster's favourite younger writers at this time were [William] Plomer, Isherwood, Rosamond Lehmann, L.A.G. Strong, and John Simpson [John Hampson], 'most of them under thirty and doing things I should like to have done'. But he does not say what they were.

When Forster was invited in 1946 to reside in King's he needed to be reconciled, at sixty-eight, to the life of celebrity that took the place of inspired writing. He was fit, capable of enduring slow Atlantic flights, of exploring the Grand Canyon on muleback, and of lecturing at Harvard, Chicago and Bryn Mawr, engagements which must often have tested his stamina. Back in England he resigned from the NCCL on a serious point of principle, broadcast his congratulations to India and Pakistan on their independence, and published his *Collected Short*

Stories. He had his own coterie, of course not identical with yet kin to Isherwood's; the Buckinghams, not writers, were near its centre, and so was the apparently charming libertine Sprott. The other necessary names are Plomer and Ackerley, talented minor figures. His relations with the fellows of his college were amiable, but he made closer ties with younger men, like P.N. Furbank and Timothy Leggatt, much later Senior Tutor of the College, both of whom travelled or went on holidays with him. Sprott seems to have been regarded with special indulgence, given the use of Forster's London flat and of money when he needed it – gifts from a donor who could now, even more readily than before, admit that he had more than he needed.

Forster and his closer friends were apparently frequent visitors to Sprott in Nottingham. There is a study of the 'extended family' they formed there in Patrick Belshaw's biographical study, *A Kind of Private Magic*; published in 1984, it attracted little notice, possibly because the quantities of dull fiction mixed in with the historical account make the product a tiresome and unreliable read. Belshaw, the real nephew of a certain Charles Lovatt, reports that he acquired three honorary uncles, uncle Jack (Sprott), uncle Morgan and uncle Ted, alias Edward Shread, socially the most obscure and least privileged of the group. Their inter-relationships, as remembered in maturity by the boy Belshaw, apparently included an educational element and the practice, or at least the discussion, of 'a kind of private magic', which meant, at least approximately, sex.

One thinks again of Forster's remarks about the value of cliques ('the clique is a valuable social device') though there is still a need, especially for artists, to be careful about what clique they join. The Apostles served him well in their way, and except in the opinions of deplorable outsiders like Dr

Leavis, so did Bloomsbury, which had more than its share of Apostles, persons of talent undoubted save by the envious – the Woolfs, Maynard Keynes, Roger Fry, Lytton Strachey, Duncan Grant, Clive Bell, T.S. Eliot, and more. Bloomsbury was in part a continuation or senior version of the Cambridge club; and possibly Sprott's community in Nottingham was another rather parodic version.

Nor did membership of such groups, any more than his membership of several London clubs, mean that Forster shunned all acquaintances who did not somehow belong. A journalist and essayist who lives into his nineties is likely to have known a great many people who were interested in him and whom it was possible and pleasant to cultivate. Dozens of them are to be found in the indexes to Furbank's biography and the *Selected Letters*; in the relatively few letters that have so far been published (at least fifteen thousand more are preserved) one sees that many were addressed to well-known people with whom he had business or desired acquaintance (for every man hath business and desire, such as it is) – an unusual but understandable proportion being Indians.

If he felt he would enjoy or profit by knowing someone, or if he enjoyed a book and wanted to thank the author, he would sometimes make the first move himself. His close friendship with the Northern Irish novelist Forrest Reid began in this way. He did not always prosper; one notable failure was his approach to A.E. Housman. It began when, in the spring of 1907, after a walking tour in Shropshire, he wrote to Housman saying that his admiration for *A Shropshire Lad* had grown with time. He neither expected nor received a reply. Sixteen years later he wrote again, thanking Housman for his *Last Poems* and explaining that he had nothing to say but simply wanted to express his gratitude. He left out his address 'to preclude any question of a reply', but Housman sent a kind acknowledgement, after which the correspondence and the acquaintance paused for five years. Forster then wrote a brief letter to accompany the gift of his short-story collection *The Eternal Moment*, as usual ending with a denial that he needed any acknowledgement. Housman nevertheless responded, but in a letter so 'absolutely hateful' that Forster, having scanned it, threw it into the fire. He was hurt but blamed himself, surely rather absurdly, for 'forcing the pace': 'I had tried for intimacy too soon.' Housman was famous for hoarding polished insults and producing them on what he considered apt occasions, of which this, in his misanthropic view, was perhaps one.

That was the end of the correspondence. Apparently Housman had taken offence at what he considered to have been bad manners on Forster's part when he was in the process of delivering the Clark Lectures. The lectures are in the gift of Trinity College, and the lecturer enjoys the hospitality of that college while necessarily in Cambridge. Forster, in Housman's opinion, did not dine in Trinity as much as he ought to have done, preferring a rival establishment, his old college, King's, a quarter of a mile away. Forster treated this story as 'a piece of Trinity silliness'. 'What a college! What dons! Offended till death because I had eaten in King's!' Housman's complaint does seem bizarre, but so does the fact that over the years these men had ample opportunity to meet had they wanted to. Forster inserted, without express acknowledgement, a reference to a Housman poem in one of the Clark Lectures, and Housman, who attended the lectures, must have noticed this; but when the lecture was over presumably made his way back to Trinity, where he noticed the guilty absence of the lecturer at dinner. A year or two later Forster happened to be dining in Trinity, this time under no obligation, real or imaginary, to do so, and found himself sitting uneasily beside Housman.

Feeling a need to say something, he mentioned that he had recently visited South Africa, and made some allusion to the Cape. Housman remarked that there was a university there. The conversation ended and they never spoke again, even when meeting by chance in a Cambridge street. It is not very surprising that Forster could feel some pain when snubbed by this sad and wonderfully gifted man, though he might have given more thought to the contradictions he embodied: perhaps the greatest living classical scholar devoting his life to editing one of the dullest and least useful poets of antiquity and at the same time himself a poet whose gloomy reveries gave such lasting pleasure, especially to young men of Forster's generation.

This experience taught Forster what he must really have known already, that creative imagination could coexist with a daunting coldness of temperament, and with a readiness to be unkind rather than considerate. When Housman read T.E Lawrence's confession that he had 'a craving to be famous and a horror of being known to like being known' he wrote in the margin 'This is me'. Forster, who profoundly admired Lawrence and who himself quietly wanted to be great, might have seen in his own person a reflection of that conflict. That Housman fell in love with a Venetian gondolier Forster might have thought enviable, though Housman's tendency to cry when publicly reciting an ode of Horace might have seemed over the top. Also Housman quite wanted to die, which was not a failing of Forster's. 'I can bear my life, but I do not at all want it to go on.' Housman would daily run up the many stairs leading to his rooms in Trinity in the hope that he might drop dead at the top. Again one detects a disparity between different Cambridge versions of the creative imagination. Yet he was, as he said, 'a egotistic hedonist', and so, in an equally quiet way, was Forster.

Of course Housman was in no sense a rival. With his classical education (second class honours, like Rickie in *The Longest Journey*) Forster would not have supposed himself more of a scholar than would be expected of a well-educated young man; he would doubtless have serviceable Greek and Latin, though he was told at King's that he had been badly taught at his public school.

When he went down from Cambridge he was almost certain he would be a writer, which meant in practice a writer of stories and novels. On the whole he tended to back away from major writers if they were at all given to experiment. Joyce, Wyndham Lewis, Gide, Upward, the rival fantasist Kafka, were dismissed or ignored. He was in his seventies when the *nouveau roman* appeared on the scene, so his age would probably have cancelled any obligation to look into it, not that he was likely to have felt one. Proust was a great exception, perhaps because he had hit upon a method not unlike Forster's own.

He was generous with his praise, and wrote letters of thanks to authors whose work had pleased him. He also corresponded with some of his early critics – with Peter Burra, for instance, and with Lionel Trilling and Wilfred Stone, author of what is still the most valuable academic study of Forster. When he liked a poem he might praise it almost extravagantly, as when he said that Auden's Freud elegy was the best poem he had ever read. It is indeed a poem of the highest class and there is no great need to complain; nor is it a difficulty that he made so much of another poem that Auden had angrily rejected from his canon. If he ignored the poets of a generation later than Auden's we may regret not having heard his views on Larkin or, say, Elizabeth Bishop, whom he might have loved.

He usually knew a great book when he saw one, hence his

praise, late in his life, for Lampedusa's *The Leopard*, which he read in Italian before the English version was available. His admiration for *War and Peace* was lifelong, and he was clearly equal to the ordeal of Dostoevsky, though in his opinion the Russian might be dangerous to English readers. It is useless to complain that he didn't do all the reading we might have wanted from him. His reports on current fiction were dutiful but superficial. They were not creative acts, the only kind that mattered.

The Ruler, the Maharajah of Dewas State Senior, as I mentioned in the third chapter, was an important figure in Forster's life. He had met Forster on his first Indian visit in 1912–13, a visit inspired by Forster's love for Syed Ross Masood, whom he had tutored in 1906. The Maharajah persuaded him to return for his second, in 1921–2, by asking him to be his private secretary. He was, said Forster, 'certainly a genius and possibly a saint, and he had to be a king'. However, 'one can never be certain of saints'. The Ruler's devotion to Krishna was practically continuous, his Old Palace was 'numinous', he was capable of ecstasy; he danced like David before the ark and undertook rigorous fasts. 'The unseen was always close to him.' He believed the deity suffered from periods of inattentiveness from which humanity might hope for his recall.

His management of his complicated affairs was disastrous. At his major festival, Gokul Ashtami, riotously and ruinously expensive and largely devised by him, 'every detail, almost without exception,' said Forster, 'is fatuous and in bad taste – a mixture of fatuity and philosophy'. Gokul Ashtami was glorious mess and muddle, to be superbly transformed in the final section of *A Passage to India*. The brilliant letters in which Forster described the chaotic celebrations and his own part in them can be read in *The Hill of Devi*. As with the state, so with the Ruler: in one perspective Bapu Sahib, as he liked to be called, had a career that could be thought crazy and irresponsible, even chaotic, yet he was loved even by officials of the Raj, who might have found him simply infuriating. 'One of the sweetest characters on earth', said Forster, who also named him as one of the most important influences on his life: a king whose mismanagement cost him his throne, a religious genius presiding over a festival of superstitious muddle, and a saint whose eccentricities western psychologists might tame by describing them – his trances, his dances, his follies – as symptoms of 'an abnormal but recognizable state'.

Whatever the diagnosis, Bapu Sahib gave Forster what he called 'the great opportunity of my life'. Writing to his mother and to other people he 'wanted to amuse', his manner is, as he says, 'too humorous and conciliatory, and too prone to turn remote and rare matters into suburban jokes'. Certainly his letters, though full of acutely noted detail, are cool and amused. One could suggest the difference between their account of the great festival and the reworking of that event in *A Passage to India* by the image of Professor Godbole no longer absurd but entranced, a wonderfully evocative vision of both Bapu Sahib's and Forster's own mystical aspirations. Yet a necessary complement of Gokul Ashtami was the clear, ordered monody of the voice of the muezzin, heard in solitude.

Forster, in a note included in *The Hill of Devi*, explains that on his 1921 visit to India he took with him the opening chapters of *A Passage To India* but 'could do nothing with them'. Back in England he was able to resume work on the novel, still calling it 'bad'. He thinks it could not have been completed without the encouragement of Leonard Woolf, but he dedicated it to Masood, later, in the important Everyman edition of 1942, adding the name of the Maharajah to the dedication. For some reason Masood stands alone once more in later editions. He had an incontestable claim as the true origin of Forster's interest in India; but the Maharajah, described by Mrs Darling, wife of Sir Malcolm who saw the Ruler through many scrapes and intrigues, as 'the most loveable, most original and most unwise man I have ever met', deserved a share of the dedication.

Without insisting too firmly on the point, Forster more than once declared *The Longest Journey* to be his favourite among his novels. As he wrote to Peter Burra, it 'is the only book which has ever given back something to the places from which I took it'. Twenty-odd years later he was still claiming, in a letter to the American critic James R. McConkey, that this was 'by far' his best book.

By this I think he means that it is the fullest demonstration of his 'method'. The plot, having to do with the consequences of a concealed adultery and inherited disease, has an Ibsen-like aspect – Forster was an admirer of Ibsen, and knew what he was doing, even to the point of inserting into the novel a defensively disparaging allusion to the playwright. His plotting is deft and telling: Gerald and Agnes kiss and he dies; Agnes and Rickie kiss in the train just as it is killing a child; so that, thinking of Lucy Honeychurch and Miss Quested on the Marabar Road and Miss Quested again in her moment alone with Aziz at the caves, one is seduced into thinking that in Forster kissing is always disastrous, or on the verge of being so. The symbolic moments often do double duty; level crossings are still dangerous and still bring death to children; Stephen is talking sense at the end when he says a footbridge is needed. But they are also forced into being a less material kind of threat, and the level crossing is one of several leitmotivs presaging death. The Madingley dell seems a benign location until Agnes invades it and tempts Rickie to enter, resembling at this moment a knight from Ariosto or Spenser tempted by the promise of sexual pleasure to abandon temperance. The text is full of allusions to certain 'symbolic moments' and other significant anecdotes, like the tormenting of the boy Vardon – a genuine instance of what Forster specially hated, providing a physical image of the school's general infliction of pain and privation. Greek myth and Arthurian legend add their senses. Demeter presides, 'shimmering and grey'; Rickie can be at times either Parsifal/Perceval or the sick king, and we can read the clue; there are mysteries whose relevance is eventually revealed, like the photograph of Stockholm, and others that are not.

Forster was always certain that clues to a hidden or other-world narrative must be available in the course of the story, little interventions serving part at least of the purpose of the Proustian *petite phrase* of which, at the time of writing *The Longest Journey*, he knew nothing, though while he was waiting for Proust he refined Meredith's method and tested the reader's knowledge of *Das Rheingold*.

Most impressive, perhaps, is what might be called the evocation of the earth, the spiritual geography. Wiltshire is not just the heart of England but the earth more generally, as if to reaffirm Ansell's thesis: the world is there, however mysterious, and cannot be seen by the likes of Agnes and Herbert. There is a pleasing assurance about the concreteness of the quotidian Cambridge in which these matters are decided, and London is not neglected. It can be said that there are, as usual, too many sermons: 'The sense of purity is a puzzling, and at times a fearful thing. It seems so noble, and it starts at one with morality. But it is a dangerous guide, and can lead us away not only from what is gracious, but also from what is good, etc.' Forster knew he shouldn't do so much of this kind of writing, but he was stubborn, and did it even more in

Howards End. In the end one gives up and accepts these passages as part of the offered bargain, as determining the tone of the whole. Some of the ethical, pseudo-religious slogans which are present in *The Longest Journey* will still be there years later in 'What I Believe' – 'the holiness of the heart's affections and the truth of Imagination' (to quote the passage correctly), 'the Beloved Republic'. Mr Failing may think his wife's conduct on her excursion to Stockholm shows that the Beloved Republic will not be brought about by love alone, yet years later the Republic appears without such daunting reservations.

So I think one can understand Forster's affection for the book. How understandable is the affection his readers continue to feel for E.M. Forster? As a guide to conduct he is valued rather as a modern version of the sincere but witty clergyman, and as a guide to literature he was for a good many years a skilful though not exciting broadcaster, his programmes much admired in India. People seemed to think Lytton Strachey's nickname for him, the *taupe*, 'the mole', was apt, but he had also the quality described by Virginia Woolf as 'manly'. He could speak out. He lived to be old and still active, an achievement that almost always impresses the public. He understood ecstasy and inspiration. He loved India, knew at first hand its delights and failings. For years he hoped that it might benefit from Jacopone's prayer – that it might be set in order. He himself, caught between two worlds and loving the old one better, might have offered the same prayer on his own behalf.

Select Bibliography

NOVELS

Arnold Bennett, *The Old Wives' Tale* (1898), *Clayhanger* (1910), *Riceyman Steps* (1924), *Elsie and the Child* (1924)

Joseph Conrad, *The Secret Agent* (1907)

Ford Madox Ford, *The Good Soldier* (1915)

E.M. Forster, *Where Angels Fear to Tread* (1905), *The Longest Journey* (1907), *A Room with a View* (1908), *Howards End* (1910), *The Celestial Omnibus* (1911), *A Passage to India* (1924), *Maurice* (1971)

John Galsworthy, *The Man of Property* (1906)

André Gide, *Les Faux-Monnayeurs* (1925)

Henry James, *What Maisie Knew* (1897), *The Ambassadors* (1903)

D.H. Lawrence, *The White Peacock* (1911), *Women in Love* (1920), *The Plumed Serpent* (1926)

Muriel Spark, *The Prime of Miss Jean Brodie* (1969)

H.G. Wells, *Ann Veronica* (1909), *Boon* (1915)

Virginia Woolf, *The Voyage Out* (1915), *Mrs Dalloway* (1925), *To the Lighthouse* (1927), *The Waves* (1931), *Between the Acts* (1941)

CRITICISM

Wayne Booth, *The Rhetoric of Fiction* (1961)

John Carey, *The Intellectuals and the Masses: Pride and Prejudice among the Literary Intelligentsia, 1880–1939* (1992)

Edward Carpenter, *Towards Democracy* (1893–1902), *Love's Coming-of-Age* (1906)

Andy Croft, *Red Letter Days: British Fiction in the 1930s* (1990)

E.M. Forster, *Aspects of the Novel* (1927)

P.N. Furbank, *E.M. Forster: A Life* (1977), *Selected Letters of E.M. Forster* (1983)

Philip Gardner, *E.M. Forster: the Critical Heritage* (1973)

Samuel Hynes, *The Edwardian Turn of Mind* (1968), *Edwardian Occasions* (1972)

Alison Light, *Mrs Woolf and the Servants* (2007)

Percy Lubbock, *The Craft of Fiction* (1921)

Edwin Muir, *The Structure of the Novel* (1928)

Jonathan Rose, *The Intellectual Life of the British Working Classes* (2003)

Sheila Rowbotham, *Edward Carpenter* (2008)

Wilfred Stone, *The Cave and the Mountain: a Study of E.M. Forster* (1966)

Lionel Trilling, *E.M. Forster: a Study* (1943)